SECR
OF THE
MOOR

A walker's guide to Exmoor landscapes

Chris Chapman · David Parker · Philip Priestley

With photographs by Chris Chapman

EXMOOR BOOKS

© Chris Chapman, David Parker, Philip Priestley
First published 1992

EXMOOR BOOKS
Dulverton, Somerset

Trade sales enquiries:
Westcountry Books
Chinon Court
Lower Moor Way
Tiverton. EX16 6SS
Tel: 0884 243242
Fax: 0884 243325

Exmoor Books is a partnership between
The Exmoor Press and Exmoor National Park

British Library Cataloguing in Publication Data
A CIP Catalogue Record for this book is
available from The British Library

ISBN 0 86183 208 6

Front cover photograph: John Podpadec

Designed for Exmoor Books by
Topics Visual Information,
397 Topsham Road,
Exeter EX2 6HD
(0392) 876800

Typeset by Exe Valley, Exeter
Printed in Great Britain by BPCC Wheatons Ltd, Exeter

CONTENTS

FOREWORD

All around me are friends who are sporty and who look with dismay at my lack of enthusiasm to join in. Some kick a ball around on Saturdays, some lift their arms with a remote gesture to their Iron Age ancestry and fling a miniature spear at the pub wall, while others ride the waves in glorified bath tubs and dream of our seafaring past. Good for them, but I don't like it!

It's not that I'm bone idle, it's just that my solitary temperament doesn't mix too well with these activities. As a photographer, the simple pleasure of walking is, at best, a visual feast and often a happy balm for the mind (though I must concede that, for some, walking means pain . . . wasn't it Churchill who said 'Why walk when you can ride'!).

When I was a child I used to stay at my grandparents' house on a Saturday night, in order to go bird watching with my Uncle Michael the following morning. He was a keen naturalist and taught me that if you wanted to see the countryside at its best, without the bustle and disruption of people, an early morning start was essential.

He would talk with great excitement the night before, but when it came to getting him out of bed – that was a different matter. Daybreak would find me making him endless cups of tea, pulling at the bed clothes and tickling his feet. With moans, yawns and groans he would eventually rise and together we'd set off on our adventure.

Those forays on to the Pennine Moors have stayed with me

into adult life and although I cannot claim to be a naturalist, they instilled in me a great love of walking. It is true some days that the effort needed is supreme. Nobody likes the steep ascent, the clammy skin or the pumping pressure as your heart takes the strain. But there is no pleasure without pain! The rewards are numerous. That physical tiredness is a sweet drug and I couldn't claim to feel anything less than sheer bliss at the end of a day's walk.

Making the television programmes *Secrets of the Moor* has been a pleasure and has rewarded me with some knowledge of what was unknown territory. Here is a landscape of untold variety, with hidden combes and rolling open space. You can trace man's endeavours from the New Stone Age right through to the present day and it needs no explanation as to why the area became a National Park.

Remember however that all land belongs to someone. Walking should do no harm and all I would ask is that when you come to explore, have due regard for the people that live here, follow the Country Code and leave no trace of your passing!

To walk on Exmoor, to enjoy it, to be confident in the lonely places, does require some preparation and equipment:

The Ordnance Survey 'Exmoor Tourist Map' covers almost all of the National Park and is useful for getting an overall picture of Exmoor. Also, as some of the walks in this book are not circular, a map is essential to indicate interesting routes by road or pathway back to the starting point. The Ordnance Survey 'Pathfinder Maps' are by far the best to use when walking. The scale 1:25000 or about 2½ inches to the mile give excellent detail. Those covering the walks in this book are sheets SS44/54 Ilfracombe; SS64/75 Lynton and Lynmouth; SS84/94 Minehead; SS63/73 Bratton Fleming and Brayford; SS83/93 Exford and Brendon Hills; SS82/92 Dulverton.

Over the years I have tried, tested, and unfortunately bought, numerous items of clothing and accessories that would enhance my love of walking. The following advice may save you money.

Thin layers of clothing, lightweight and easy to carry, are your best bet. These should be buttoned or zipped at the front, both for the convenience of nature and temperature control.

2

Thermals are wonderful and although not the height of fashion can be a life saver (just remember that your partner may not tolerate then in bed!). In the depths of winter wear a hat as most of your body heat is lost through the head.

Don't wear trainers! Strong footwear is essential and many a twisted ankle has been caused through disregarding this advice. My first boots were of Eastern bloc origin and felt like a pair of lead-lined clogs, but today's technology produces leather boots which are strong and light and, although the best are expensive, they should give years of service.

Waxed cotton jackets have become a British institution, but unless you fancy walking around in a mobile Turkish bath avoid them. There are now a number of fabrics which 'breathe' and a great variety of styles and colours are available. The fashion conscious will always go for dayglow but remember that the wildlife you may want to encounter will see you first!

A waterproof lightweight jacket (and trousers) can be supplemented with a polar fleece. The fleece isn't windproof, but has the effect of a fur lining when worn underneath. Cotton shirt and trousers (not denim) are a good bet and cushioned-soled, mixed-fibre socks are an ideal precaution against blisters.

A rucksack of 35–45 litres is an ideal size and as with boots, it is false economy to buy a cheap one. Go to a shop and ask them to fill one. Then, disregarding the sniggers from other customers, have a good tramp around the floor. It took me over an hour to decide on mine, but my shoulders have been forever grateful!

Finally, the small but often forgotten essentials: a first aid kit for peace of mind, a lead for the dog if he turns a deaf ear, a whistle in case you can't walk anymore (and coins for the telephone if you think you can), a small torch, and chocolate for comfort and energy. Last but not least a compass and map ('Pathfinder' series) to tell where your going. Never underestimate the weather even if you are blessed with the instinct of a homing pigeon. Cold and mist has a nasty habit of dampening the spirit and obscuring the view ahead!

Chris Chapman

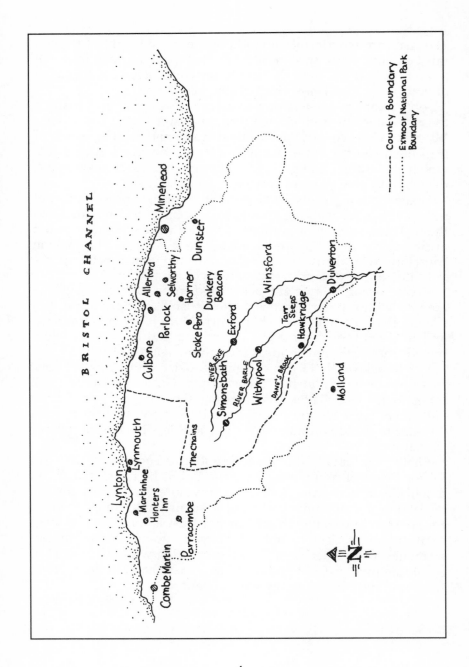

BRISTOL CHANNEL

Minehead
Dunster
Allerford
Selworthy
Horner
Porlock
Culbone
Stoke Pero
Dunkery Beacon
Exford
Simonsbath
RIVER EXE
Withypool
RIVER BARLE
DANE'S BROOK
Winsford
Tarr Steps
Hawkridge
Dulverton
Molland
The Chains
Lynmouth
Lynton
Martinhoe
Hunters Inn
Parracombe
Combe Martin

N

County Boundary
Exmoor National Park Boundary

4

EXMOOR

A WALKER'S PARADISE

If you walk across the Chains, high on Exmoor, you might think that this boggy and often inhospitable grass moor is a wilderness, untouched by the human hand. But you would be wrong. Even this, the most isolated area of the Exmoor National Park is littered with evidence that men and women have shaped the landscape over many centuries.

The discovery of a 'henge' close to the farm at Woolhanger tells us that people lived and worked this part of the moor more than 4000 years ago. Barrows and standing stones are clues to the settlement of the high moor by Bronze Age settlers who farmed and tended their stock from 3000 BC. Perhaps the most famous of all Exmoor's relics, the Longstone, is here, standing majestically at the head of a stream. Further down the valley is a ruined farm at Radworthy. The name tells us of its Saxon origins, that people farmed here before the Normans invaded England in 1066.

Carry on for half a mile and you reach Wood Barrow Gate. This seemingly inconsequential hedge and wall is in fact the boundary of the Royal Forest of Exmoor. The Forest was perhaps established by the Saxons and certainly appropriated by the Normans. It was a domain reserved for the king to hunt. The boundary was perambulated every seven years and, in many places, stones called 'Mere Stones' marked the border between the Forest and surrounding common or wastes. The track at Wood Barrow Gate, insignificant now, was important during the

Middle Ages when farmers drove their sheep along it into the Forest, on grazing let to them by the Forest Warden. A little way further and Pinkworthy (pronounced Pinkery) Pond looms out of the mists. No natural pond, this expanse of water was excavated by two hundred Irish labourers in the 1820s. The farm further down the Barle valley but with the same name, Pinkery, was also a nineteenth century creation. Both were part of the Knight family's efforts to 'tame' the moor after they purchased the Forest in 1818.

Today Pinkery is no longer a working farm. It is owned by the Exmoor National Park Authority. Exmoor was designated a National Park in 1954. The National Park Authority has the task of protecting and preserving the natural beauty of the landscape and promoting the enjoyment of the region by the public whilst having due regard for those who live and work within the Park. Their headquarters is at Dulverton in a building that was once, appropriately perhaps, a workhouse!

The Exmoor National Park covers 265 square miles or 170 000 acres with about two-thirds in Somerset and the balance in North Devon. At its heart lies the ancient Royal Forest: a high, grass moorland of 20 000 acres that belonged to the Crown from Norman times until sold in 1818.

The fascination of Exmoor lies in its varied landscape. The coast stretches for 35 miles from Minehead to Combe Martin with 900 feet high 'hog's back' cliffs, some of the highest in Britain. There are 47 000 acres of moorland, divided equally between heather and grass. Woodland covers just over 17 000 acres, half of which is broad-leaved with 7000 acres of 'ancient' woodland. There are 3400 miles of hedgerow, over 300 miles of rivers and major waters, plus hundreds of lesser streams and three impounding reservoirs. There are 700 miles of bridleways and footpaths. More than half of Exmoor lies between 1000 and 1600 feet above sea-level with Dunkery Beacon at 1704 feet the highest point. Much of Exmoor is privately owned, but the National Park Authority now owns 11 000 acres, the National Trust over 17 000 acres, the Forestry Commission 3000 and there are 12 000 acres of registered common land.

The plant and wildlife of Exmoor is just as varied and interesting as the landscape. The local Natural History Society has recorded more than a thousand flowering plants, over 200 different species of birds with 106 nesting each year, over 1000 different butterflies and moths, some of these the rarest in Britain, and hundreds of lichens (sure indicators of the purity of the air). In fact, the lichens of the 900-acre Horner Wood are recognised as of international importance. Exmoor also has 40 species of mammal including the badger, fox, hare, dormouse, rare bats, and the wild red deer, pride of the National Park. Over 1500 red deer live on Exmoor, and though scarce on the western edge, you can be almost sure to see them in the Dunkery area and around the woodland fringe of the Horner Valley. Fallow deer, and an increasing number of roe deer also live within the Park. The Exmoor pony, one of the ancient little horses of the world, roams over much of the moor.

The landscape, wildlife, history, the farming interest of sheep and cattle, the lovely villages and the people, these and much more make Exmoor a walker's paradise. And walking on Exmoor can be great fun as well as healthy exercise: fresh air on the face and in the lungs, a sense of freedom from everyday cares, breathtaking views, the sudden, unexpected sight of deer and moorland birds, the glorious pattern of heather, gorse, grass and sedge, the delicate colour of wild flowers, the sound of running water, and the ever changing light and shade racing over the hills. But the walker misses much unless he looks beyond the obvious – beyond mere scenery to the reality of Exmoor's development over the centuries which, under close scrutiny, the landscape will reveal.

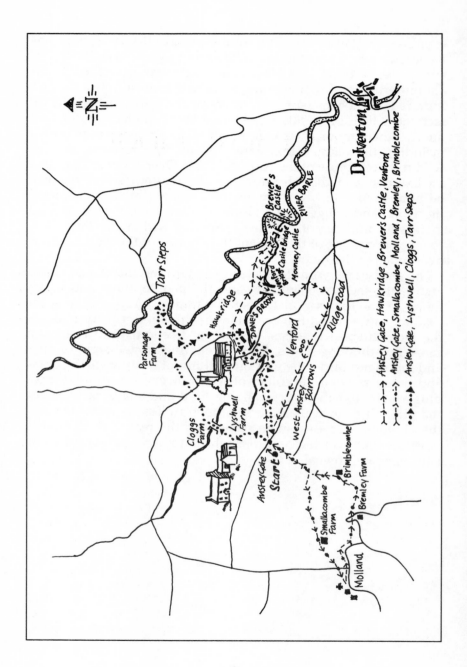

THE

SOUTHERN RIDGE

Even though much of Exmoor lies above 1000 feet there are three distinct tracts of high land. South of the River Barle a protecting bastion runs for 15 miles from Shoulsbarrow Common to Five Barrows (with a high point of 1618 feet), along Fyldon Common and on through Molland Common, Withypool Common and West and East Anstey Commons. A central range starts in the west at Chapman Barrows, on to the Chains rising to 1598 feet, and on across the middle of the old Royal Forest to Dunkery Beacon. Then there is the coastal range from Great Hangman above Combe Martin to Selworthy Beacon, many places along the way rising well over 1000 feet high.

The walks described in this section will take you along part of the southern ridge, relatively easy walking, and with marvellous views across hill farming country, open moorland, and into combes with fast running waters.

From the open roads on this ridge there is a wonderful sense of being on top of the moor. And there is an equally powerful feeling that others have been here before. The ridge road is home to many of the finest Bronze Age barrows on Exmoor: those at East Anstey Common in the east, and the collection at Five Barrows just beyond Kinsford Gate south of Simonsbath. There is a great deal of evidence to point to the fact that this road is a route dating back 3000 years. Many such ridges were followed by Bronze Age settlers, providing relatively dry and open going at a time when the undrained valleys were much more difficult to negotiate than today.

In the area to the west of Dulverton the ridge road runs out of beech hedgerows into the unfenced commons of Anstey and Molland. A cattle grid at Anstey Gate divides the two commons. To the north is the Dane's Brook and beyond it the clear outline of Brightworthy Barrows, Withypool Hill and Winsford Hill. Still further the distinctive Dunkery Beacon is visible. To the south the Moor falls away quickly. The valley below is that of the River Yeo and the plains which divide Exmoor from Dartmoor – visible quite clearly on a fine day. It is an area for good walking. There are clear views and an abundance of wildlife. On the common there are Exmoor ponies, in the wooded valleys deer harbour. Skylarks, buzzards and other birds are in evidence. Herons and kingfishers patrol the Dane's Brook itself. The woods to the north of Anstey Common are a haven for butterflies and wild flowers in the spring, the best time of the year to experience the delights of this area.

Anstey Gate, Hawkridge, Brewers Castle, Venford – 8.5 miles

This is a circular walk. It begins at the Cattle Grid at Anstey Gate on the road from Dulverton. Map reference SS835298.

Anstey Gate to Hawkridge – 3 miles

The gate is marked on the Ordnance Survey map as Anstey Gate but known to local people as Molland Moor Gate.

There are numerous paths from the gate across West Anstey Common heading in the general direction of the Dane's Brook. The name has nothing to do with the Danes and before 1800 it was called 'Dun's Brook' – 'stream from the hills'. This common has a long history but what happened between 1967 and 1987 is as fascinating as anything that went before. Over those twenty years, long, expensive and often acrimonious legal battles were fought over the registration of the common. It was finally registered in 1987, with six owners and eight commoners. The commoners have the right to graze a total of 1233 sheep, 183 cattle and 36 ponies on the area, although if all these rights were exercised neither animals nor common would survive a year. There is a full account of the attempt to enclose West Anstey Common in *The Essence of Exmoor* by Victor Bonham-Carter (Exmoor Press).

The path crosses the part of the common known as Anstey Rhiney Moor, running down the southern slopes of the Dane's Brook. The views across to the north are wonderful and represent classic Exmoor. Here is a landscape, not of villages but isolated farmsteads. Most of the farmhouses are sturdy, south facing dwellings – the winters can be fierce at this height. This is sheep country. The Exmoor horn is the recognised stock and the foundation of the economy of the farms that you can see before you at Lyshwell and Cloggs to the left and Zeal to the right. The landscape reverberates with sheep, whether it is lambing in the early spring, shearing in late spring and early summer, or dipping and markets towards the end of the summer.

This is also red deer country. Look out for them on the common and out across the water at Shircombe and Zeal Brakes. They graze in the silage fields of Shircombe and are very distinctive – particularly through field glasses.

The path falls to the river at the Dane's Brook, the boundary between Devon and Somerset, and follows the river along its course to Slade Bridge, two miles from Anstey Gate. The brook, often a trickle at the height of summer, becomes a roaring torrent in winter, fed by the south-westerlies bringing rain and northerlies snow. Walk quietly along this stretch and you might see one of the herons that feed on the tiny brown trout in the stream. In the oak, beech and alder trees are nuthatches and treecreepers.

At Slade Bridge there are traces of a leat leading off to an abandoned farm a little way downstream. In 1327 a 'Nicholas at Slade' farmed 36 acres here. Leats are channels taken of off a stream or river with the flow being controlled by sluice gates. They served a variety of purposes. Some were dug to take water

Longstone Combe, looking towards Hawkridge

to spring grasses to secure an early growth and save on winter feed. Others, like this one low down in a river valley, provided power to farm machinery or a mill wheel. Perhaps this leat fed a mill for grinding corn for the parish of Hawkridge, the village on the hill on the other side of the Brook.

The path now crosses the bridge and follows Slade Lane towards Hawkridge. The bridge itself has an interesting history. The clues to it are to be found by studying the structure from below. You will see that the original bridge was only about 8 feet wide and built for packhorses. Until the mid nineteenth century the packhorse was the only means of transporting goods around Exmoor. During World War II Slade Bridge was not big enough for American tanks so they knocked down the upstream wall and widened it. This and other parts of Exmoor were used by allied forces as a training ground during the war.

The walk goes up the road from the bridge, past the entrance to Zeal Farm where 'Elias of Sele' lived in 1257 and was fined four shillings for sowing two acres with corn in the king's Forest of Exmoor. The name Zeal is probably Saxon for 'great house'. Another 100 yards and the path goes right up through grass fields signposted to Hawkridge.

Hawkridge has a village hall, post office and an interesting church, but no pub, no school and only a few houses. In spite of this the village is still holds a traditional 'revel' on August Bank holiday each year on Zeal Farm land, and amongst other events is an occasional week-long exhibition of 'Old Hawkridge' in the village hall.

Turn right into the village and you will pass the workshops of Tom Lock, one of the prime movers behind the exhibition. This is no ordinary workshop. Tom, like his father and grandfather before him, was the village carpenter, but in retirement he has taken to another craft – the sculpting of deer antlers.

Next door to Tom Lock's workshop is the parish church. Parish churches are lovely places to roam around and this one is no exception. You can read about it in the church leaflet. No one knows the date of the founding of the church but its proximity to Tarr Steps suggests it was Saxon. It has some Norman features including a font and south doorway. The churchyard was the venue for the Swainmote Court held between 15 May and 18

Tom Lock and his antler chair, Hawkridge

'The family have been in Hawkridge since 1840 at least. My great great grandfather was called Tout. Great grandfather came to work for him, to learn the trade – carpenter. Eventually he married his daughter and took over the trade.

It was natural for me to become a carpenter. Just like my father and his father. Trouble was I'd just learned to make a wheel when tractors came in and carts went out of fashion. Making wheels just died out.

I started working with antlers as a hobby. People used to bring me antlers. I made all sorts of things, whistles, key rings and candlesticks, even a chair.'

June to administer the Norman Forest Law governing the king's Royal Forest of Exmoor. The Free Suitors of Hawkridge with those of Withypool were obliged to attend (see note on the Free Suitors in the Withypool-to-Simonsbath walk).

The churchyard suggests it is a place with a sense of history, the gravestones revealing a continuity of community in the farmsteads in the area.

Hawkridge to Castle Bridge – 2.5 miles

The route passes the church and ignores the sign to the left for Tarr Steps. It carries on along a lane called Row Lane to a gate and continues across open countryside, Hawkridge Ridge. Take the path to the left signposted Mounsey Castle and Castle Bridge.

This is a marvellous stretch of countryside with stunning views. To the left the ridge drops away to the River Barle and in front the path slopes down through woodland to the Dane's Brook. You may well see red deer here too and a variety of birdlife: buzzards overhead, and in the woods tawny owls, nuthatches, treecreepers and woodpeckers, with redstarts, wood warblers and pied flycatchers during the summer months.

The path drops steeply down to the Dane's Brook, the woodland carpeted with bluebells in late May. This is a delightful section, the light streaming through the overhanging alders, ash and oaks, making a pattern of light and shade on the water.

Just before the junction with the River Barle the path passes below Brewer's Castle, the smaller of two Iron Age forts in this area. This one is named after a William Brewer, who from 1216–1222 held land in Hawkridge parish. He was one of a few privileged folk with the king's licence to hunt deer in the Royal Forest. A path leads up to the earth ramparts of the castle. Now it is well wooded, but 2500 years ago it would have been cleared of trees allowing wide views of the river. These castles, as they are called on Exmoor, were defensive fortifications and places of refuge for the early settlers and their stock. The second castle here is on the other side of the river and is called Mounsey Castle. It is much more imposing but is on land managed by the Somerset Trust for Nature Conservation and permission is needed to visit it.

The woods here are part of Exmoor's ancient woodland, but coppicing shows that they have been shaped by human activity over many centuries. The practise of coppicing involved cutting the oaks down quite close to the ground. This rarely kills the tree and new growth soon appears which, twenty years or so later, can be harvested. The bark was used for tanning leather, and the timber very often for charcoal. Charcoal burners were a race apart, moving on from place to place but needing to live in the woods close to their work. Shallow pits in the ground often reveal their burning sites.

In its final few yards the Dane's Brook flows beneath Castle Bridge, named, of course, from the overshadowing Iron Age forts, to join the River Barle. This is a lovely spot, the furthest point of this walk, and a convenient place to break for a rest and picnic. In the late spring there are marsh marigolds here, and the delicate wood anemone – a certain sign of ancient woodland, and there is evidence that the rarely seen otter lives along this stretch of the Barle.

Castle Bridge to Anstey Gate – 3 miles

The return path to Anstey Gate is a yellow waymarked walk and follows the northern side of the Dane's Brook. On this stretch there has recently been extensive felling and tree work. The woods suffered a lot of damage in winter storms in 1990 and the National Park workers have been busy tidying up and planting new trees.

This is a very popular place to watch deer. They come down to the brook to drink and in the heat of the summer to wallow in the mud. The numbers of wild red deer running on Exmoor have increased in recent years and they are magnificent animals to watch and photograph.

Like so much of Exmoor this is hunting country where the staghounds, kennelled at Exford, pursue the deer through woods and over moorland. The National Park Authority has no official view about hunting, it neither encourages nor discourages it. But, almost everyone else on the Moor does have a view. Aside from the pro- and anti-hunting lobbies there are those who are concerned about the balance on Exmoor between male stags and female hinds.

A mile from Castle Bridge the path divides. Take the left fork and cross the wooden Venford Bridge and follow the signs for Venford and East Anstey Common. 'Venford' is literally a ford across a fen or marsh. When the path leaves the wood and crosses Whiterocks Down there are some areas particularly at the head of springs or streams that are marshy and soft underfoot.

About a mile beyond the bridge cross the road and strike out across East Anstey Common. If you are in this area in the late afternoon on a sunny day, look out for the prehistoric field systems and boundaries which reveal themselves so well in the late afternoon sunlight. This is particularly so looking across the Dane's Brook valley towards Zeal and Hawkridge. It is possible to pick out field boundaries and tracks no longer used, and evidence of past ploughing. In more recent times hedges were built by prisoners from the Napoleonic war in the early years of the nineteenth century.

Farmers like Philip Veysey from Venford Farm are involved in farm conservation schemes. These schemes, funded by the National Park Authority provide grants to the farmers to help restore traditional farm features such as banks and hedges, ponds and wet areas. It is all part of a move to conserve the countryside rather than farm merely for profit.

On reaching the ridge road Anstey Gate is still two miles off, and the moorland road, 1100 feet up, can be followed for this last section. You will be passing several Bronze Age barrows dating back 3500 years, evidence of earlier settlement on this high land. It is known that the climate was warmer then and suitable for growing crops. Certainly they buried their dead up here, though perhaps only the tribal chiefs. Could they possibly have imagined that thousands of years later these simple remains of their culture would prove so fascinating for twentieth century man?

Close by Anstey Gate there is a shrine of a different kind. It is a 13-ton boulder, a memorial to Philip Froude Hancock, brewer and hunting man who died in 1933. One wonders whether Froude Hancock was seen as a latter day tribal chief?

Two More Walks From Anstey Gate

1. Anstey Gate, Lyshwell, Cloggs, Tarr Steps – 8 miles

This walk includes two working farms on Exmoor: Lyshwell Farm and Cloggs Farm.

Take the unfenced road, with a beech hedge on your right, from Anstey Gate north to Lyshwell Farm. This will take you through a gate. Here the hedge ends and the route surface changes to a wide farm track running along the side of a grass field. In 100 yards you will see an old quarry on the left, and, on the right, ruins of an abandoned farm called Landcombe. In addition to the usual farm buildings this had an ash house – the ashes were carefully collected as fertiliser – and in the wall of the house a beehive facing the heather on Anstey Common. These were not uncommon features in old Exmoor farmsteads.

The way drops steeply down to Redford Water and then climbs steeply out to skirt Lyshwell Farm. This is part of the Molland Estate and is farmed by Raymond Davey and his wife. Over the crown of the hill you may spot the grass-covered foundations of another long-deserted farm. This was North Lyshwell, and clearly there was a much larger farming community here in the past.

Many of the old farming ways and customs have gone, but they are still remembered by the older farmers of the district. Evening light still reveals shadowy outlines on the hillsides of barns, paths and hedges.

The route to Cloggs Farm is over fields and is waymarked in red. There is another steep drop to the Dane's Brook, crossed by a stout wooden bridge, and a stiff climb to Cloggs where the path is diverted round the buildings. By the farm gate a stream running through a shippon feeds a series of gullies cut into the

Barbara Bawden, Cloggs Farm

David Bawden and his father Fred, Cloggs Farm

'There have been seven generations of Bawdens at Cloggs Farm. We farm in what you would call a traditional way. We've got about 300 acres and we keep Exmoor horn sheep and Devon cattle crossed with Charolais. Mother and father are here with his two sisters, Gwen and Barbara and then there's me and my wife Pearl.

We are part of a new scheme run by the Exmoor National Park, The Farm Conservation Scheme; they are trying to keep things on this farm the way they were in the past' slopes of the meadow. Little sluices would have been opened or closed to divert the water any way the farmer wanted it to flow and because it ran through the shippon it would have enriched the meadow with manure. A very simple and yet effective way of fertilising a field.

Cloggs is farmed by the Bawden family. They have been there for generations and today son David and his wife, Pearl, farm with father Fred, mother Jane and aunts Barbara and Gwen. This Exmoor farm, 1000 feet up, is one of those leading the way back to a traditional approach to farming with support from the Exmoor National Park conservation scheme.

The Bawdens go one step further. Gwen organises guided walks around the farm for curious and enthusiastic visitors. The walk takes one-and-a-half hours and ends with a cup of tea. It's well worth the visit and details of the dates and times of the guided walk can be found in the *Exmoor Visitor* published by the Park Authority. In fact a whole range of guided walks are advertised in this free publication.

Just before Cloggs there is a signpost to Hawkridge and Tarr Steps. This will take you across grass fields on to the track coming up from Shircombe Farm, and to the road at Tarr Post. Turn left here and continue for 100 yards and then right on the tarmac road for a mile to the edge of Row Down Wood. Turn left into the wood and then right as you come out from the trees and into a lane to Parsonage Farm. Just beyond the farm the route drops through fields to Tarr Steps half a mile away.

Tarr Steps is an impressive structure, a stone causeway 180 feet long, considered by many to be the finest example of a clapper bridge in the country. Historians argue about its origins – some consider it to be medieval, others date it much earlier. Its recent history, however, is just as interesting. It was destroyed in the great flood of August 1952 but the stones were recovered and the bridge was rebuilt by the army. Tarr Steps has become one of Exmoor's big tourist attractions or 'honey pots' as they are called. It encapsulates all the dilemmas of tourism and its impact on the moor. The National Park has built a car park on the north side of the river to try to deal with the increasing traffic which weaves its way through country lanes designed for packhorses and carts. The footpaths along the Barle suffer erosion from the weight of feet and much of the wildlife deserts the immediate area for more quiet pastures. There is a cafe just above the riverbank. But what can the authorities do? Should they build more car parking, widen the roads and provide tourist information? Or, should they try to deflect the car drivers from this area and seek to direct them to alternative spots which are still attractive but under less pressure from visitors? A real dilemma.

Approaching Tarr Steps on foot from the Hawkridge direction you do not experience too many of the problems. There are no car parks on this side and the woods and riverbank are relatively tranquil.

From Tarr Steps follow the Hawkridge road for one mile then right at Penny Bridge, up through the woods and left on to the Two Moors Way and then one mile into Hawkridge. Keep following the signs 'Two Moors Way'. This will take you over the hill and through the farmsteads of East and West Hollowcombe and down to Slade Bridge. Once across the bridge take the path to the right and follow the river for half a mile. Then strike out from the river across the common to the ridge road and Anstey Gate: the end of the walk.

2. Anstey Gate, Smallacombe, Molland, Bremley, Brimblecombe – 6 miles

This walk is quite different from the others. Indeed it takes the walker out of the National Park. The walk runs south from the high road and into countryside which lies between Exmoor and Dartmoor. If the weather is fine and the day clear there will be no problem in seeing the hills of Dartmoor to the south-west.

The landscape is different too. Once off the common it is a patchwork of small fields, villages, water meadows and country churches. More like the classic rural landscape of the image makers.

From Anstey Gate take the path south on the Molland side of the cattle grid with the hedge on your left. Follow the path over moorland to the south running through Anstey Gully, a combe with hawthorn and rowan trees, the bottom full of rushes and the usual stream. Continue south-westwards to Smallacombe on the National Park boundary and then on the road for a short distance and then on the well-defined track for Molland

The village is worth a visit for the church alone. One of the loveliest and unspoilt in the whole area. The Victorian improvers somehow left it alone. It is well described by Hazel Eardley-Wilmot in her book *Yesterday's Exmoor* (Exmoor Books). The local pub – The London Inn – is described by S H Burton in his masterly work *Exmoor* (Hale). Both books are full of information for the walker.

From the village follow the road east to Latchgate Cross and then the path to Bremley. Now up the road for a short distance and a path to the right will take you to Whitley Farm. The way goes through the farmyard, and then follows a stream northwards to Brimblecombe Farm. Continue on this path through fields and up on to the open moor to Brimblecombe Hill and Anstey Gate is on your right.

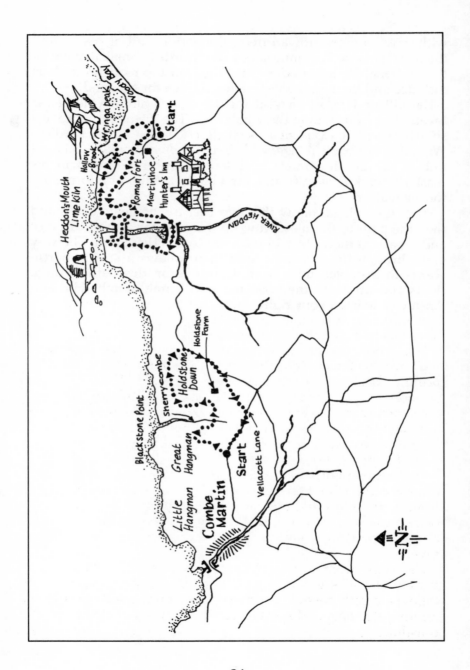

Woody Bay
Wringa Peak
Start
Hollow Brook
Heddon's Mouth
Lime Kiln
Roman Fort
Martinhoe
Hunter's Inn
RIVER HEDDON
Holdstone Farm
Sherrycombe
Holdstone Down
Blackstone Point
Great Hangman
Little Hangman
Combe Martin
Start
Vellacott Lane
N

24

3

THE COAST FROM COMBE MARTIN TO WOODY BAY

The 35 miles of coast from Combe Martin in the west to Minehead in the east is a walker's dream. Most of the area is high cliffs, only Porlock Vale breaking this pattern, and a good deal of the coast is owned by the National Trust. These two facts have ensured a minimum of development.

This whole coastal region is particularly striking, much of it well over 1000 feet high. The cliffs of the 'hog's back' formation begin their descent to the sea some way inland. The long slopes support a variety of vegetation, sometimes all the way down to the shore. Many are too dangerous and inaccessible for walking, although the existing paths in the area are well defined and safe. This in many ways is the least known and the least accessible part of Exmoor.

The area supports many kinds of bird life. Nesting sea birds return to the cliffs between Woody Bay and Heddon's Mouth from April to July, buzzards and kestrels hunt in the woods and open areas. You may well see a peregrine diving down the cliffs at great speed in pursuit of its prey, or hear the deep croak of ravens.

The coast from Combe Martin to Woody Bay has a wide variety of walks to suit a wide variety of tastes. The two that follow are both possible in an easy day's outing and are circular, offering stunning and spectacular views of different parts of the coastline.

1. Great Hangman and Holdstone Down – 7 miles

Starting point at map reference SS598472

This walk includes the two great summits of this area – Great Hangman is 1043 feet and Holdstone Down, the highest coastal hill in the South West at 1143 ft. As one would expect the views are really outstanding.

The walk begins at the junction with the track to Girt Farm in Vellacott Lane, a mile and a half east of Combe Martin. Walk up the track and bear right at the bungalow – climb steadily for a mile to the moor and the field boundary. Here you join the coast path, signposted with an acorn symbol.

It is worth taking a detour to the left to see the view from the top of Great Hangman. It is truly breathtaking. Below in the foreground is the smaller but no less dramatic, Little Hangman. Beyond is the inlet to Combe Martin and in the far distance Ilfracombe, Hartland Point and Lundy Island. To the east Great Hangman sweeps towards Sherrycombe and Holdstone Down rises magnificently on the other side.

On the seaward slope of Great Hangman lie the remains of a fascinating aspect of past mining activities in the area. You can approach these by following the signs for Blackstone Point. Notice the workings in the side of the cliff on the path. They could be mistaken for caves but are in fact iron-mining adits. In Elizabethan times the area was famous for its silver, but in the last century iron ore was the main mineral, when men dug it out of the side of the cliffs and hurled it towards the sea to be picked up by boats on the beaches. What a wild and desolate spot in which to earn what must have been a very meagre living. But the coast did provide a living to all sorts of people. Women picked seaweed laver from the beaches below Great Hangman and Little Hangman. This was used in the kitchen but a good deal was sent to London stores. On the top of the cliffs the whortleberry grows well and is highly valued for pies and tarts. Until the Second World War whole families would come out during the season and harvest the wild purple berries, and children had a special whortleberry holiday. At one time this area, now deserted save for the few walkers, would have been busy with all sorts of economic activity. Yet there are only a few scars left on the landscape to remind us.

On the Holdstone Down side of the valley are the outlines of field enclosures and what looks like a drift-way from the open moorland into the fields. It would probably have been used by the shepherds on the Down to bring stock in, another reminder that at one time the cliffs were busy with farming.

The landscape here is part of the classic coastal heath of Exmoor. Different types of heather flourish. The common heather or ling dominates and with its soft deep pink looks absolutely stunning in late August. It combines with the golden yellow flower of the western gorse to create a beautiful, natural kaleidoscope of colour. Darker, deeper and a richer purple are the flowers of the bell heather which appear earlier and last longer; you can find cross leaved heather here too. This plant loves the wetter areas. The Heather is under severe threat in many parts of the moor and Great Hangman is no exception. For years farmers have burned it – swaling they call it – to produce fresh young shoots. It is far less extensive than it was at one time, and is threatened by the spread of bracken. The bracken looks lovely to the walker, apple green in summer, rust in the autumn, and it certainly has its champions. But most people believe that the uncontrolled spread of bracken on the moors presents an ecological catastrophe and on this stretch measures are taken to control it. You can see the results on Great Hangman and on the slope toward Sherrycombe. The landscape is a patchwork of shades of green, where the heather has been swaled in different years and the bracken cut.

It looks a beautiful and natural landscape, yet thousands of years ago the area was wooded. It was the clearing of these woods by Bronze Age settlers that gave the shrubs and herbs a better chance to flourish. In the past it was largely farmers who shaped the landscape but since 1971, when much of the area was bought by the National Trust it has been under their careful management. The aim is to preserve the habitat as it is now. Even the stock-grazing rights are drawn up with this in mind. Horses are grazed because they will nibble the gorse and so help

27

keep it under control – a few cattle because they keep the mire open and preserve a micro-habitat for insects and bog plants.

The walk follows the coast path east across the deep sided gorge called Sherrycombe and towards Holdstone Down. At the mouth of the combe a waterfall leaps 70 feet over the edge onto the beach below. It is a superb sight but the walk down to it is off rights of way and it is difficult and dangerous. The best way of seeing it is to take a boat trip from Ilfracombe. This is one of many coastal falls on Exmoor – a product of the 'hog's back' cliffs, and part of the very fabric of this area. It is typical of the only area of the moor that man cannot tame – the only part of Exmoor that remains a true wilderness.

There is a steep climb up to Holdstone Down and if you want to experience the view from the top, the highest point along this part of the coast, the climb is even longer. Is the view worth it? Well one man clearly thought so because in the 1920s he bought up land on the hill hoping to divide and sell it to prospective buyers. Plots were organised, many were staked out and numbered and a few of the stakes remain. He built a road – that is still there. However, not enough people looking for a holiday home thought Holdstone Down appropriate. Can we blame them, for it is very bleak. The plan failed and the rest, as they say, is history.

The alternative to the climb to the top of Holdstone Down is to follow the path on the seaward side of the Down. On the way you will pass one or two bungalows – built high on the hill with the moor sweeping before them to the cliffs and sea. They have wonderful views but must take an awful battering if there is a south-westerly or westerly wind.

The path back to the start of the walk follows the road inland for one mile as it runs around Holdstone Down. A path to the right is signposted Holdstone Farm. Leave this path after 200 yards and take the track to the left. This will bring you back to Vellacott Lane. Turn right and follow the road back to the track at Girt Down a distance of just over one mile.

Just before you arrive back at the track to Girt Farm there is a track to the left marked Knapdown Farm. It is worth taking a short diversion down the lane to see some of the remains of the silver mines of the Combe Martin district. Take the righthand track at the junction and follow the path called Corner Lane and you will see the chimney of the old engine house. Further down the lane are the remains of Harris's shaft, part of the Old Combe Martin Mine. Shafts were sunk to tap the four lodes of silver and lead which ran down the hillside and under the village. This mine closed in 1848, a few years earlier than Knap Down Mine which remained open until 1868, breaking a mining tradition which dated back to the thirteenth century at least.

Continue down the lane for another 150 yards, when it joins Watery Lane. Follow Watery Lane and then into Pentice Lane.

All these lanes cut deep into the soft shale, perhaps because of their heavy use by carts, or the effect of rainwater. The fields above the lanes have strips running down in diagonal fashion. Some were allotments worked by miners, a tradition replicated in many part of the country.

The lanes here are typical of those around Combe Martin. Their banks are home to a variety of ferns, mosses and lichens.

At the junction of Knap Down Lane turn right and the road takes you back to the start of the walk at Girt Farm.

2. Woody Bay to the Heddon Valley – 6 miles

Starting point map reference SS675485

This walk begins at the car park above Woody Bay. It follows a wide path round the higher part of the coast and then drops down to Hunter's Inn in the Heddon Valley. The return is by a narrower and lower path nearer the sea.

It is in truth a very popular walk – at least in the height of summer. But if you are able to enjoy this area outside school holidays or in mid week you will be amazed how few people you will meet on the route. It is still the case that most visitors to these parts don't stray too far from their cars – perhaps they are afraid they might lose them! This is a pity but for the slightly more adventurous walker there is a good chance you will have even this most popular of routes to yourself.

Walk down the road from the car park for 200 yards and turn left on the road to Woody Bay. As the road bends sharply to the right take the path over a stile next to a five-bar gate and follow it along the woodland edge for half a mile. You will notice how well made this path is. It was, in fact, built a hundred years ago as a carriageway for horse-drawn vehicles from Woody Bay to the inn in the Heddon Valley. If you look carefully you will see the stone watering troughs built for the horses.

After a while the oak woodland ends and the path stretches out to open countryside. Look for the wild thyme, rock stone-crop and Welsh poppies which grow here. The cliffs fall away gently on the right and in places the lower path – the return leg – can be spotted.

The path bends round the Hollow Brook gorge and in a quarter of a mile a sign points the walker up the side of the hill to Martinhoe Signal Station. Scramble up the path cut into the grassy slope and you are soon in a field. Here you will be able to pick out the parapets of what was a Roman signal station – the small hillock-like boundary of which is still clear enough on the ground. You will be able to see up and down the coast and across to south Wales just as the soldiers of the Roman garrison could nearly 2000 years ago. But what would they have been looking for? Archaeologists and historians who have excavated the Martinhoe site believe that the signal station was intended to give warning of invasion or attack from the sea, from tribes of Celts from South Wales called 'Silures'. An impending attack would have been spotted early and ships warned so that they could put to sea to protect the coastal villages and settlements. It is likely that the camp was occupied only in the summer even though proper dwellings were constructed. Perhaps even Silurian tribes might find winter on Exmoor a less than exciting prospect. There is a good account of the excavations along with some of the finds at the museum at Barnstaple which is well worth a visit on a separate occasion.

The carriageway continues along the upper part of the cliffs for another mile and then swings inland above the river Heddon. Stonechats, whitethroats and linnets nest on the scrubby slopes.

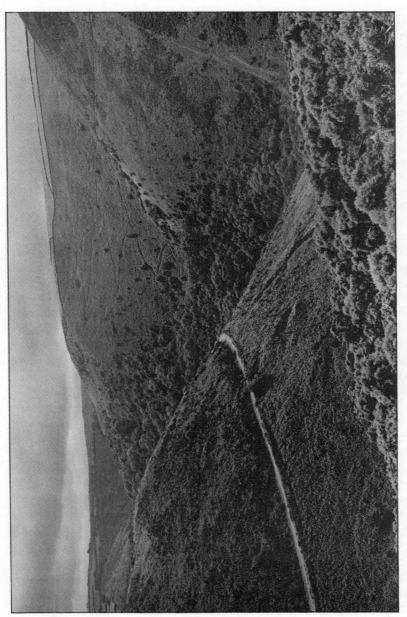

Heddon's Mouth Cleave

31

Finally the path winds through oak woodland into the shelter of the valley and Hunter's Inn.

Look at the woods as you walk through the oak and ash canopy. Can you tell that the National Trust, the owners of the area are continuing a practice carried on for two hundred years – managing the wood? For a long time this oak wood was coppiced for timber that was used for charcoal. Charcoal was an important fuel up until the Industrial Revolution. Its use declined in the nineteenth century but the timber was always needed. Short poles for fencing, thicker ones for props in pits – in fact the last commercial use of the beach at Heddon's Mouth was to take cargoes of timber from here to South Wales for the mines during the First World War. Oak bark was used in the leather industry until the end of the nineteenth century. Many small towns close to the Somerset and North Devon coast had tanneries up until fifty years ago.

So the woodsmen ensured that oak was available. Every twenty years or so the oak would be cut at the base, 'coppiced', and then allowed to sprout from the bottom. Other species would be cut down altogether, though hazel was coppiced for hurdles and thatching pegs. A real monoculture. As the use of the oak died so did woodland management, and from the turn of the century until quite recently nothing was done to this woodland. The results are apparent on one side of the path – look down into the valley and you can see that the woodland is weak – the oaks thin, other species like beech and ash struggle for light and ground cover is poor.

Look upward and it is a different picture. On this side the National Trust has undertaken extensive work to thin and clear some of the weaker single oaks. Light has been brought into the woodland and other species – ash, rowan and hazel have been encouraged alongside the oak. The woods are home for a variety of birds; buzzards now common across Exmoor nest here with warblers, nuthatches, redstarts and green wood-peckers amongst others.

The woods are a welcome break in the landscape. Follow the path right down and you will see a smaller track joining the carriageway from the right. This is the lower path, the return journey to Woody Bay. Before you take the route you might want to carry on down the carriageway through the five-bar gate, and to the open valley floor of the Heddon River.

Hunter's Inn is a popular hotel and close by is a shop selling bric-a-brac and gifts and with a snack bar. There is also a large car park and during the summer months it is used by the many tourists who visit the valley. Many come on coaches, part of a North Devon tour. Most people do not walk very far from the car park. Some will stroll down to the mouth of the river, fewer still will stroll in the other direction back up the valley even though there are some really excellent woodland walks. Most stay around the riverbank and browse around the shop and Hunter's Inn.

If you have time on the journey back it is worth taking a short detour following the path along the river to Heddon's Mouth. There are routes to the sea on both sides of the river and on the way down look at the meadows lying in the bottom of what is reputed to be the warmest valley in North Devon. These are traditional hay meadows, and are now managed for conservation by the National Trust. The Trust is providing a habitat for the fritillary butterflies in these meadows. There are Dark Green Fritillaries, Small Pearl-Bordered and the rare High Brown Fritillary here, plus lots of flowers, especially marsh thistles, knapweed and buddleia, beloved of butterflies. Hedgerows have been kept wide, and the trees thinned out. Marshy areas have been left alone so that the marsh marigold and meadow-sweet can thrive. The whole area is delightful and particularly so in the late spring. Come here in mid June and you can see all this and much more. The woods are home to various ferns – the male, lady and buckler ferns along with hart's tongue fern thrive here. At one time they were collected and sent to London, decorating the homes of the well-to-do during the Victorian fern craze.

Caroline Giddens, of the Exmoor Natural History Society has written an excellent book *Flowers of Exmoor*, a checklist of all the plants growing in the Park. It is excellent value for money and a good companion to any walker interested in flowers and plants on the moor. The Society has also produced booklets on the birds and the lepidoptera as well as a complete *Flora and Fauna of Exmoor*.

33

Heddon's Mouth is about a mile and a half downriver from Hunter's Inn. The beach is shingle and pebble but it is one of the few places along the Exmoor coast where it is possible to land a boat, a hazardous task nonetheless. But, despite the dangers, ships unloaded cargoes at Heddon's Mouth in the last century, crewed by men up to no good! This was smugglers' territory.

A dark night in 1786 saw a confrontation between smugglers and custom men at Heddon's Mouth. It was one of the rare occasions when the smugglers were surprised. Although the customs officers seized twenty ankers of spirit (an anker is 8½ gallons) and thirteen bales of tobacco they did not apprehend the smugglers – who all absconded in an Irish wherry. The crew of the *Hope* were not so lucky. In May 1799 smugglers landed 96 ankers of brandy before moving further west, heading for Watermouth. But the vessel ran on to rocks and all hands were lost. The little church at Martinhoe was probably used to store smuggled spirits. In fact the parish register has an entry against a certain Dick Jones who died a the age of 103, 'last of the smugglers'. It obviously did him no harm!

There was of course honest trade in the bay too. Limestone and coal were landed at Heddon's Mouth as they were at many of the little inlets and bays on the coast. Brought from South Wales and burnt in kilns dotted all along this stretch of coast, the lime that resulted was carried away from the area by packhorse up into the fields to combat the acidic soils. The lime kiln here has been restored to something like its original condition, and is a good example of the type found along this coast.

The route back to Woody Bay is by the lower of the two coast paths. Follow the path back from Heddon's Mouth and cross the river on the small wooden bridge. The coast path is marked clearly and signposted Woody Bay. Follow this path to the edge of the wood where it turns to the left and climbs steeply up the gorse-covered slopes. In under a mile you reach the rocks of Highveer Point. It is tremendous vantage point with views back up the valley and the water meadows, the beach and lime kiln, and in both directions along the coast for miles.

Continue to follow the path eastwards and in a mile-and-a-half you arrive above Wringapeak. This is a really fine stretch of

Cyril Manning, birdwatcher, near Wringapeak

Cyril Manning works as a volunteer for the RSPB. For forty years he has been counting and recording birds on this coast.

'I think it's a way of life really, I love it, there is nowhere else I'd rather be. My plot for the seabird census is Lynmouth to Heddon's Mouth, about five miles. It has colonies of razorbills and guillemots and since 1954 the fulmar has been breeding here. They spend nine months out on the Atlantic and don't come onto the cliff at all except to breed. They are very sociable birds packed shoulder to shoulder on the cliffs. They stay here from about the third week in May to the end of July. The razorbill will bring in anything up to 8–10 fish a day crosswise in its beak.

When the chicks are about three weeks old they flutter down to the sea. One of the parents stays with them to teach them how to fish and they don't come back to land until next year, as an adult; that is their breeding cycle.'

coast for the ornithologist. It is helpful to have field glasses and essential to come here in June or July for the best birdwatching. These cliffs, inaccessible to man, are home to thousands of nesting birds.

If you come here in June you will be amazed not just by the seabirds but by the cliffs themselves: they are like a wild rock garden. Wild thyme, rock stonecrop, lichens, pennywort, all thrive here amidst heathers and gorse.

Just behind Wringapeak the path crosses Hollow Brook, another of the coastal waterfalls. Shortly beyond the falls the sessile oaks take over from the heathers, broom and gorse for a mile until the path spreads out on to the road to Woody Bay. You turn right to get back to the car park but don't leave the area without walking down to the sea at Woody Bay.

One cannot do better than quote local author Harriet Bridle, who in her book *Woody Bay* begins with this: 'Woody Bay sweeps in a magnificent curve, its grandeur strikes and haunts the eye and heart and mind. The eye traverses rocks and boulders and the flat topped cliff of Crock Point, swings round and climbs to the pinnacle of the sheer, and sometimes vertical, hog's backed heights of 800 feet or more.'

Visit the bay and you will get the picture. It is approached down the lane through oak woodlands. Sessile oaks dominate as they do everywhere along this coast but there are interesting rare species, yew and whitebeam amongst them. Red campion, foxglove, ragwort, orchids and sorrel are among the many plants that carpet the ground. Look carefully and you will also see two plants that are the scourge of the bay and cause a great controversy. Himalayan knotweed is reputed to have taken hold when a clergyman sprinkled seeds along the path of the old Lynmouth to Barnstaple railway line. Ever since, residents and the owner of the area since 1965, the National Trust, have been trying their best to get rid of it. But with roots going down to forty feet it is not that easy.

At least everyone agrees that Himalayan knotweed is a pest. The same cannot be said for the rhododendron. This 'weed' is the cause of great argument in Woody Bay between some of the 'locals' who like the flower and the National Trust, and others,

36

who hate the effect the plant has on native species. The National Trust is clearly winning this particular argument. The sound of the waves breaking over the rocks, the drumming of the great-spotted woodpecker and the laughing call of the green woodpecker are regularly interrupted by the drone of enthusiastic National Trust chainsaws, wielded by equally enthusiastic National Trust volunteers, as they fight to save another wood.

Before you reach the beach the path passes a row of white-washed cottages on the left. Today they are holiday houses but at one time local folk lived there. Some were lime burners' cottages and sure enough on the beach itself there is a lime kiln and even the rusting remains of a railway running into the sea, used, one presumes, to land limestone and coal on the beach.

Once on the beach itself look to the left, to the west. At low tide you will find the foundations of a pier built in 1895 by a local entrepreneur, who turned out to be a crook, by the name of Benjamin Green Lake. The pier was to have been 100 yards long, although early financial problems cut that to 80 yards, still big enough for the large pleasure steamers that Lake hoped to attract to the bay. He had big ideas to turn the area into a tourist trap. The trouble was he did not have enough money of his own so he borrowed from other people – without their consent. The whole episode ended in tears – or, in Lake's case, jail when he was sentenced to twelve years. He died in 1909, but at least he outlived his pier. That could not survive the storms of 1900 and was eventually pulled down in 1902.

Across the other side of the bay is a swimming pool also built by Lake. The changing room he erected for 'ladies' has gone. Women have to do the same as everyone else if they want to swim – dance about with a towel around their body.

But it is the natural features of Woody Bay that linger longest in the memory. The setting is perfect, high 'hog's back' cliffs clothed in woodland with a beautiful coastal waterfall as the centrepiece. In the words of Ms Bridle: 'The colours of Woody Bay are forever changing according to the time of day and mood of weather. The rose pink of the dawn sky switches to the ethereal white light of the evening. The sea, varies from a soft, quiet millpond to an angry, stormy monster.'

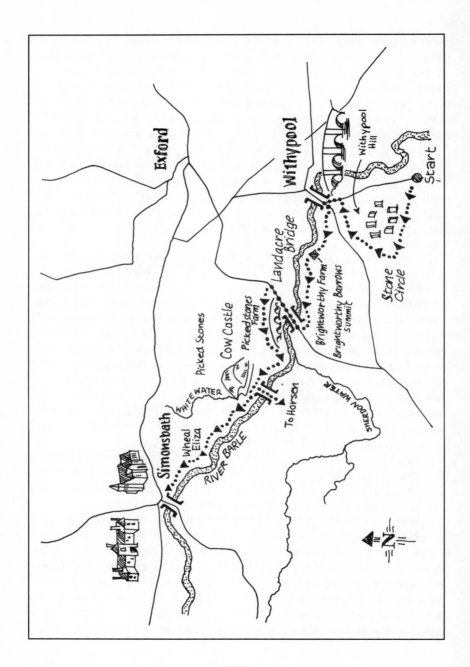

4

THE

BARLE VALLEY

Withypool to Simonsbath – 8 miles

The River Barle rises at Pinkworthy Pond in the heart of the Chains and makes its way through Exmoor via Simonsbath, Withypool and Dulverton. It leaves the National Park near Brushford where it joins the River Exe at a spot called Blackpool.

The river flows through many phases of Exmoor's history. There are Bronze Age settlements on the hills and Iron Age forts in the valley. It is spanned by two of the most famous bridges on the Moor; Landacre Bridge and Tarr Steps. The whole area is an absolute delight for the walker. The beauty of the valley is unsurpassed.

This chapter describes a walk from Withypool to Simonsbath with guidance on shorter circular walks on the way. The distance is about 8 miles from village to village.

Withypool Hill to Landacre Bridge – 4 miles

Starting point at map reference SS47338

This walk begins by a cattle grid on Worth Lane a mile south of Withypool, and above the wooded valley of the River Barle. Worth Lane is part of the Two Moors Way linking Dartmoor with Exmoor. From the cattle grid take the broad track leading westwards across Withypool Hill and Withypool Common. (Please

Withypool Bridge

note, however, that although Withypool Common is often used as an open access area, it is privately owned and the permission of the landowner and commoners should be obtained before departing from rights of way.).

At first there is a characteristic earth and beech hedge on the left, but this soon gives way to the open moorland of Withypool Hill. Stop for a moment and look round at the extensive views across Westwater Allotment and on to Hawkridge. The summit of Withypool Hill is 1306 feet high. On its south-west facing slope, some 200 yards from the top, is one of Exmoor's stone circles. Comprising about thirty stones, none of them more than two feet high, it is reckoned to be Bronze Age, circa 1000 BC, but little is known about the people who erected it. They left no written records; we don't even know the language they spoke. All they left behind are these stone circles, rows, hut circles, and burial mounds or barrows containing human remains and pottery.

It is best to skirt around Withypool Hill and to take the path that bears to the right, eventually joining the public road just above the village of Withypool. Walk down the hill and, for a pleasant diversion, cross over the bridge and into the village with its inn for refreshments, church and shop. The bridge with six round arches is only just over 100 years old, and before this there was a packhorse bridge 100 yards upstream. All the stone for the existing bridge was quarried and carried to the site by local farmer John Milton. He was the first allowed over the bridge and the whole village turned out to watch the event. Withypool long had connections with the Royal Forest and three inhabitants named as Dodo, Almor and Godric are mentioned as foresters in Domesday Book. In the last century the population was twice its present size, and now, in the words of writer Victor Bonham-Carter, it is 'hanging on by its eyelashes'.

The visit to Withypool has been an aside. The path resumes beside the bridge on the southern bank of the river, and continues up the Barle passing below the farmland of Knighton on the left and through the farmyard of Brightworthy. These are ancient farmsteads and the holders in times past were Free Suitors of the king's Royal Forest of Exmoor. Altogether there were fifty-two holdings to which free suits were attached, thirty-seven in Withypool parish and fifteen in Hawkridge parish.

Their duties, neglected under pain of fine, were to drive the Forest on horseback nine times a year for stray cattle and sheep, to perambulate the Forest boundary once in seven years, and to attend the twice yearly Forest Court. Only two excuses for non-attendance were recognised: wife be in travail with child, and dough be leavened to be baked that day. In return the Free Suitors received free pasture within the Forest for 140 sheep, five horses, and a small number of cattle and pigs. They also had the right to cut turf, heather and fern for their own use only, and to fish the rivers.

Having passed through Brightworthy walk along the track that brings you to the open moorland of Withypool Common. There are twenty registered commons within Exmoor National Park; Brendon Common of 2138 acres is the largest, and Withypool Common of 1891 acres is the next biggest. These are the only two commons on Exmoor with Commoner's Associations which can exercise some control over stocking rates and management of the vegetation. All common land has an owner of the soil; but there are others, usually neighbouring farmers, with certain rights on the common. On Exmoor these rights are usually of pasturage, turf and fishing. The owner of Lanacre Farm is Lord of the Manor of Withypool and owner of the common.

Here, below Brightworthy Barrows, 1404 feet up and the highest part of the common, you will see the need to manage the sward. Much of the heather has disappeared and moor grass (*molinia*) has taken over. This is due in part to over-grazing, swaling, and more recently to the ravages of the heather beetle. Swaling or burning is necessary from time to time to get rid of old or leggy heather and encourage new growth, but where it is overdone there is often an invasion of bracken, rushes and moor grass.

In the vicinity of the barrows you are likely to encounter Exmoor ponies, almost certainly the herd belonging to Fred Milton, a notable breeder of the ponies. His family have lived in Withypool since the seventeenth century and Fred was born at Weatherslade Farm where he has spent all his life. It was one of his forbears who greeted the parson in the church one Sunday morning with the request 'Do'ee, sir, preach from the steps for the old goose is abroad in the pulpit; her's come cruel hard on hatching, and must no how be disturbed.'

42

**Fred Milton and his wife, checking over their Exmoor ponies,
Weatherside, Withypool**

*'Father bought this place in 1905. I was born a year later and I've been here ever
since.*

*Years ago, in Grandfather's times we kept ponies 2 and 3 years old and then
sold them. They went over to Wales underground as pit ponies. Well, we sold
the last ponies for pits in 1919. I was glad when it stopped but they were well
looked after you know. Now lots of them go for riding ponies or pony driving.*

*The number of wild ponies on Exmoor has decreased – now we are down to
two groups on the Common. Wild herds have disappeared because they've been
cross bred and then you lose your pure breed mares, the hardy pony that will
winter out quite happily.'*

At present there are only seven registered herds of pure bred Exmoor ponies within the National Park; five kept by private owners, and two by the National Park Authority, one on Larkbarrow and the other on Haddon Hill. They are all descended from a herd of twenty collected off the Royal Forest by Sir Thomas Acland when the Forest was sold by the crown in 1818. The special features of the pony are its small but sturdy size, general brown colour but lighter flanks and underparts, the mealy muzzle and a bright, prominent 'toad' eye, short pointed ears, and complete absence of any white markings.

Approaching Landacre Bridge you are near the site of the ancient Swainmote or Forest Court. This was held twice a year, once at the bridge here, and once in Hawkridge churchyard, afterwards retiring to the Royal Oak Inn at Withypool.

Where the path meets the road, rather than heading immediately for the bridge, turn left and walk a few hundred yards up the hill. On the way you will see a well-used track leading off on the right of the road. This leads to Sherdon Water, a major tributary of the Barle, and to Ferny Ball, home to one of Exmoor's most redoubtable residents, Hope Bourne. She has lived on Exmoor for a greater part of her working life, alone and self-sufficient. She has witnessed Exmoor in all its moods, and has written about it with an enthusiasm and respect for what she sees as the last wilderness (Hope Bourne, *Living on Exmoor*, Exmoor Books), *see page 91.*

Sherdon Hutch is the meeting place of Sherdon Water with the Barle. The junction forms a deep pool where the waters swirl between high banks. For many years sand martins nested here, but they have been driven off in recent years by summer bathers. The ground is generally boggy and full of marsh plants like marsh woundwort, bog St. John's wort, bog asphodel, heath spotted orchid, meadowsweet, valerian and two insectivorous plants – the round leaved sundew and the rare western butterwort.

Retrace your steps down the road and return to Landacre Bridge. This is a fine five-arched bridge, and quite an old one. There are records of repairs to it in 1610 and 1621 and as a

Above the Barle, looking towards Withypool Common

45

county bridge a rate to pay for the work was raised on the Hundreds of Carhampton and Williton. The archaeologist Hazel Eardley-Wilmot has traced the medieval road linking South Molton to Exford and Porlock and found it crossing the Barle at Landacre. It is probable that its construction was connected with the packhorse trade in wool from South Molton to ports on the Bristol Channel.

Crossing the bridge proceed up Landacre Lane, pass Lanacre Farm (minus the 'd' in the spelling, for in the thirteenth century it was 'Longacre') and as soon as you come to the open moor you will see a broad track on both sides of the road. The right-hand track goes down Kitridge Lane to Withypool two and a half miles distant.

If you want to continue with the walk to Simonsbath turn left from Landacre rather than right. Fortunately, the path here is wide and heather is well mixed with the western gorse. This is a low-growing gorse, not much higher than the heather, but walking through it can be quite painful. They flower together towards the end of August making a patterned carpet of yellow and purple.

Landacre to Simonsbath – 4 miles

Here you can look back across the whole of the valley of the Barle sweeping across the foreground; Landacre Bridge is superbly located. Beyond the valley is Brightworthy, Woolcombe Allotments and Ferny Ball. This view alone makes this route worthwhile.

A mile along the route from Landacre Lane the path drops through the contours of Bradymoor down to the Barle and then through a stile and gate in a beech hedge boundary. This insignificant looking hedge is in fact part of the 35 mile boundary of the Forest of Exmoor which, after being in possession of the crown for 900 years, was sold in 1818 to John Knight, a Worcestershire ironmaster. One of Knight's first tasks was to build a wall round his new estate, partly an earth bank topped with beeches, and partly dry-stone walling. John Knight had a nursery for the young beech saplings behind his house at Simonsbath, now the Simonsbath House Hotel. The hedges were superb shelters as well as boundary markers and remain so today. They have become part of Exmoor's distinctive character. The impact on Exmoor of John Knight and his son Frederic was enormous and the path from here to Simonsbath – the end of this walk – encapsulates a range of their endeavours.

The walk carries on through the gate and a plantation of conifer trees. They are totally out of character in this valley – difficult walking too in wet or muddy weather. There is one compensation: the edge of the plantation is home to wild raspberries and if you walk this area in the late summer they make a delicious harvest – literally fruits of the forest – but remember to leave some for the birds.

The track through the conifers is under half-a-mile long and breaks out to the Barle at a footbridge with a path which leads back to Landacre Bridge via Horsen and Sherdon. This bridge makes a circular walk from Landacre easily achievable in a day and what a delightful spot the place is. Montbretia with its distinctive orange flower has escaped from gardens upstream and spread for miles along the river. This is one of many flowers found here in July and August. Dippers and grey wagtails may be seen near the bridge. The whole area is refreshing after the walk through the woodland.

A stream coming down from the north is called White Water. This is also crossed by a small footbridge and just beyond is a conical mound known as The Calf, and behind this a much larger mound called Cow Castle. This is an Iron Age defensive fort with a rampart near the summit – like Mounsey and Brewer's Castles further down the Barle below Tarr Steps. The Barle stands out superbly and it is easy to see why the ancient people used places like Cow Castle and other Iron Age forts on the Barle. The rivers and valleys would have been important communication and trading routes and these hill tops would have been easy to defend; when danger threatened. A local legend credits the building of Cow Castle to a band of hardy moorland pixies, and it was long known as Ring Castle.

From Cow Castle there is a choice of ways to the end of the walk in Simonsbath. For the high ground with views south across the valleys it is possible to take the path up White Water to Picked Stones. This route is commonly used but is not a right of way or permissive and is not waymarked. The permission of the land-owner should be obtained before following it.

A more interesting route is to follow the riverside path to Simonsbath. A mile upstream from Cow Castle you will find the remains of the Wheal Eliza copper and iron ore mine and a derelict miner's cottage. Wheal Eliza is another of the hundreds of relics of the influence of the Knight family on Exmoor. This particular one was part of the plans of Frederic Knight to restore prosperity to the family after the crippling costs of agricultural improvements on their land.

The mine was not a success. It was worked from 1846 to 1855 by which time over £10 000 had been spent on the project for just a few tons of ore. The story of Wheal Eliza is well covered in Roger Burton's book *The Heritage of Exmoor* (privately pub-lished, 1989), though the Exmoor National Park has erected an information board on the south side of the river for those who prefer their information 'on the spot'. The board also tells of Exmoor's most horrible crime. On 7 January 1859, William Burgess was hanged in Taunton, convicted of the murder of his daughter Anna-Maria. Her body had been hidden in Wheal Eliza. The mine was pumped dry and her corpse found at the bottom of the shaft.

What the walker can now see of the mining operations is the entrance to the main shaft and the remains of a miner's cottage on the north bank. Looking across the river it is possible to pick out the leat cut out of the hillside – used to bring water to a 25 foot water wheel which pumped water out of the mine. The wheel housing is still visible though the wheel itself has long since disappeared.

The miner's cottage at Wheal Eliza lasted much longer than the mine, for it was used by the Knights and the subsequent owners of the estate, the Fortescue family, to house shepherds who looked after what was known as the 'mines herding'. Shepherds had been brought down from Scotland with their sheep by Frederic Knight – part of his plans to improve the way the estate was managed. The last shepherd to live in the cottage was a descendant of the Scottish shepherds. He was William Little, son of perhaps the best of all the Exmoor sheperds, Jack. Jack spent all his life working on the Exmoor estate, the last fourteen years at the mines herding. His daughter, Margaret, who now lives in Simonsbath remembers those year well: 'There were seven of us altogether. I was born at Badgworthy Cottage and we moved to Simonsbath when I was seven years old so that I could go to school. Father went to the mines when my uncle was killed by lightning – I got married from the mines. It was very remote, we kept chickens and a pig for bacon and made our own butter. All our stores were delivered to us once a month by horse and cart, including paraffin oil for the lamps – there was no electricity.'

A quarter of a mile upstream from Wheal Eliza is a natural mound called Flexbarrow, planted with conifers at the turn of the century. From here for a mile to Simonsbath runs the course of an old railway constructed towards the end of the First World War for transporting spruce and larch from the Flexbarrow plantation to Simonsbath. Here it was prepared in the saw mills in the village. The logs were hauled across the river to the railway on the south side. The line crossed the Barle close to the junctions with Halscombe and then ran on to Simonsbath by way of the fields below Birch Cleave Wood and the meadows, to the saw mills in the village. Look for traces of the railway over the final mile of the walk into Simonsbath.

The path to Simonsbath follows the northern bank of the river. Here it is narrow, twisting and hemmed in beside the steep slopes. Like many of Exmoor's rivers it is a paradise for anglers in search of the brown trout. If you want to read about the Barle and other Exmoor rivers you cannot do better than refer to *The Waters of Exmoor* by Noel Allen (Exmoor Press).

The final stretch of this walk to Simonsbath is through a wood named Birch Cleave Wood, although the trees now are beech, planted in 1850 by the Knights. The village is really no more than a collection of cottages, a few new houses, a pottery and a church, built in 1856 by Frederic Knight, where he, his son and wife are buried. Simonsbath was a 'company town' – the

The grave of Sir Frederic Knight and his family, Simonsbath churchyard

Knights built many of the cottages for their workers, provided a church for their spiritual needs and a school for the children. The only really outstanding building in the village is the large Simonsbath House Hotel. This was originally the first house built within the Royal Forest and was erected by James Boevey in 1654. He had bought the Forest from the Parliamentarians in 1653 for £6857 but had to hand it back, without compensation, when Charles II returned to England in 1660. Boevey, like all the Crown's representatives in the Forest before him, made his money by charging local farmers for grazing. He was detested by those farmers because he doubled the charges for pasturing, and he spent a lot of time and money in court over arguments with his 'neighbours'. Boevey was a well-known man in his day and there is an account of him in John Aubrey's *Brief Lives* of 1690.

If you decide at the end of the walk that you need refreshments you could try the cafe behind the Simonsbath House Hotel. It is name after Boevey, the most infamous Warden the Forest had. But don't let that spoil your cup of tea.

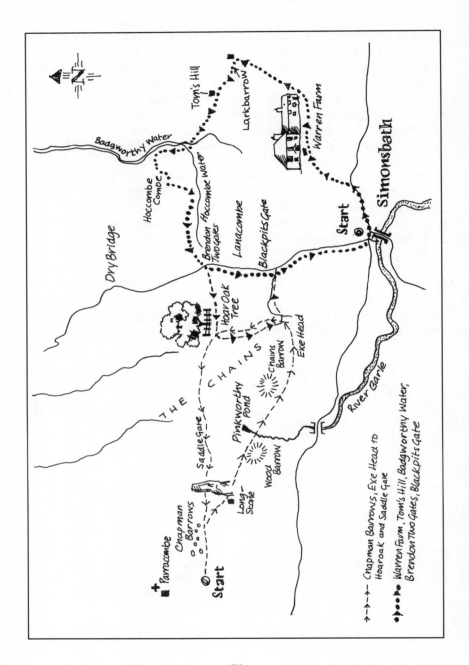

5

THE HIGH MOOR

Each person will have their own special places within Exmoor's varied landscape. For some it is the magnificent 'hog's back' cliffs, particularly in late August when the heather and gorse spread a glorious pattern of purple and yellow. Others prefer the long river valleys of the Barle, Exe and the Lyns, or the quieter combes of Chetsford and Weir Water. For others it is the shady woods of Horner and Hawkcombe, or one of the many lovely villages: Allerford, Bossington, Winsford or Exford. But there are those whose first love is the high moorland of the old Royal Forest, more remote, wild and unpredictable than any other part of the National Park. Unique too, in that it is almost all moor grass, with deersedge and rushes.

The Chains, between Lynmouth and Simonsbath, lie at the heart of this high moor. Dramatic, but perhaps not so dramatic as when Thomas Westcote wrote in 1630 'how fiery dragons have been seen flying and lighting on the barrows'. A Master of Staghounds and Member of Parliament speaking of the area said, 'I assure you that I would far sooner be anywhere on Exmoor, except the Chains in the thickest fog, than in the House of Commons.' Yet to be on the top of the moor, to know its varied moods, light and shade racing over the hills, swirling clouds and sudden mists, is an extraordinary and unique experience.

There are numerous walks across this central high moorland. A walker can spend a pleasant summer afternoon tramping from Brendon Two Gates into Farley Water valley and on to Hoaroak

Water, or a very long day walking from Chapman Barrows, across the heights to the open landscape of Larkbarrow, above the Exe valley.

The walks included in this chapter can all be enjoyed without the need of overnight stops but the weather and the ground underfoot can be very variable and change quickly. It is therefore advisable to have sturdy footwear and clothes to match the climate, and something to eat.

1. Chapman Barrows, Exe Head to Hoar Oak and Saddle Gate – 12.5 miles

A long circular walk from Chapman Barrows across the spectacular lush watershed of Exmoor.

Chapman Barrows to Pinkworthy Pond – 3.5 miles

One way to approach Chapman Barrows, the start of this walk, is to take the small unmarked road off the A39 between Lynton and Blackmoor Gate, just before the village of Parracombe. (The map ref. is SS673454). The lane leads in a no-nonsense and direct way to a gate and then no further – a result of the enclosure of Parracombe Common in the nineteenth century. At one time, a trackway linked Parracombe with Challacombe and like so many of these tracks, often originated by sheep or drovers, it fell into disuse when the car and tarmac conspired against it. An alternative route is from Goat Hill Bridge (map ref. SS724405), on the B3358 midway between Simonsbath and Challacombe, then north over Broad Mead to Wood Barrow.

The Parracombe approach is marked 'Two Gates' on the map and from here it is a short and rewarding walk across the open common to the eleven Bronze Age mounds called Chapman

Barrows. However, please note that there is no right of access here, despite it being a commonly used route.

These barrows are believed to be the resting places of tribal chiefs a thousand years before Christ. Two have been opened and both were found to contain internal chambers and human bones. We do know that in those days the climate was warmer than today and Bronze Age people settled the higher ground on the moor. Most of the evidence of Bronze Age activity (and there is a great deal of it on Exmoor with undoubtedly more to be discovered, stone circles, stone rows, standing stones, cairns and barrows), is to be found on or near the hill tops on the warm southern or western slopes.

Standing at Chapman Barrows it is possible to see a number of other barrows. Looking east, there is a clear thin chain of similar mounds: Longstone Barrow, Wood Barrow and Chains Barrow. Five Barrows is prominent to the south. But it is not only barrows that the walker can see, for this is one of the finest views on Exmoor. On a clear day Barnstaple Bay, Hartland Point and Lundy Island are visible to the west, Dartmoor and Bodmin Moor to the south and Dunkery stands clear in the east. A breathtaking sight.

A fence along the north side of the Barrows runs west/east and separates the unenclosed common on the south from the enclosed and improved fields to the north. On both, sheep, the core of the Exmoor economy, abound.

Ahead of you is the Longstone, 9½ feet high and the largest of Exmoor's standing stones. It lies in a shallow hollow between Chapman Barrows and Wood Barrow, close to a spring which is the modest start of the River Bray. There is a well-worn path from Chapman Barrows across the grass moor to the Longstone and on to the Wood Barrow. It is worth sticking to the path, since the ground is marshy on either side, even at the height of summer. On this bleak, high moorland, more than 1500 feet up, the Longstone gives the impression of a solitary figure. Noel Allen, the naturalist, thinks that this gives a clue to the naming of Chapman Barrows. At one time this area and its isolated farmsteads would have been served by the lonely chapmen or pedlars, selling their wares to the farmers' wives. Were those

The Longstone on the Chains

women and men reminded of the chapmen when they looked across the moor and saw the Longstone?

The rough path continues on to Longstone Barrow to Wood Barrow and Wood Barrow Gate. Here it crosses what, at first sight, appears to be merely a farm gate, but if you look closely, you will see a clear track. This was one of the north/south routes on Exmoor. It was important as a packhorse trail which up until the late nineteenth century was the only way of getting around Exmoor. There were no roads suitable for wheeled vehicles. This route linked Lynton to Challacombe and North and South Molton. Wood Barrow Gate also marks the boundary of the ancient Forest of Exmoor.

Once inside the Forest (there are no trees, 'Forest' in the old days meant 'waste land') the walk continues south-east over rough ground,to the first of many of John Knight's attempts to shape the Exmoor landscape, Pinkworthy Pond. The pond may look natural but the earthen dam was in fact built by two hundred Irish labourers in the 1820s.

Pinkworthy has an eerie feel about it, perhaps because it has been drained twice in the past to look for bodies. It has been the focus of some controversy and even today folk still argue about why it was built. Roger Burton, author of a recent work on the Forest, has an interesting theory. He suggested that Knight built the pond to feed a canal (a reservoir rather than a barge canal) which was to have run in an easterly direction to a point above Simonsbath. Sure enough, close by the water, on a path towards Pinkery Farm there is the bed of a canal. Burton calls the pond and the canal 'the greatest enigma to come down to us from John Knight's early days' and thinks that it was John Knight's intention to build a railway from Porlock to Simonsbath to transport lime to improve the acid soil of his peat moors. Water would have been needed to power an incline railway to raise trucks up the steep slope out of Simonsbath. The pond would have provided the water for the canal which in turn would have fed the mechanism for the railway. It is an interesting theory and there are clues in the landscape to support it. Before you leave the pond take a look at the flow of water through a tunnel on the north side. This is where Burton thinks Knight expected to link the pond to the canal.

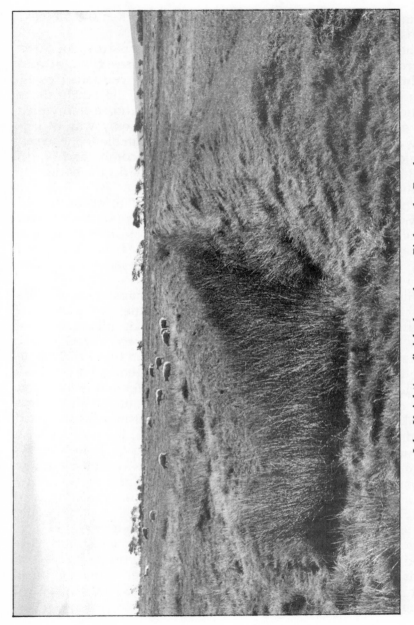

John Knight's unfinished canal, near Pinkworthy Pond

Pinkworthy Pond to Exehead – 2.5 miles

The path continues east across the Chains to Exe Head for about 2½ miles. On the way a small track to the left leads to Chains Barrow, 1598 feet up, another single Bronze Age barrow. Less spectacular than Chapman Barrows, it is surrounded by ugly and rusting barbed wire, which according to a sign is designed 'to keep out stock'. In this it is singularly unsuccessful. But why bother anyway. They seem to do the Barrow no harm.

The sense of being on the 'watershed' of Exmoor is reinforced at Exehead. The River Exe rises amongst the soft rushes and bog plants close by the path before meandering first east and then south to be joined by the Barle below Dulverton. Yet only a mile or so north the combes and their rivers all flow north to the Bristol Channel. At one time Exehead must have been busy with the traffic of packhorses. It is the crossroads of yet another north/south route across the moor, this one between Lynton and Simonsbath.

Between Exehead and Blackpits there is evidence of other Knight enterprises. On the northern slopes of the infant Exe there is a second canal. Its route is clear in the sedges and rushes and has been traced by Roger Burton. It runs from below Exehead following the contour of the Exe valley to Warren Farm. It passes by the farm, opposite the canal dug from Pinkworthy Pond. The two canals were in all probability part of John Knight's plans for a Simonsbath to Porlock railway. It is easy to imagine how Knight might have totally transformed so much of Exmoor had all his schemes come to fruition.

Exehead to Hoar Oak – 1.5 miles

From Exehead the path turns north and follows the old Simonsbath to Lynton packhorse route. Here the walk crosses the watershed of Exmoor and leaves the top of the Chains via Chains Valley Combe. The path then crosses Hoaroak Water which flows out of the beautiful but austere Long Chains Combe on the left. A hundred yards further on are the remains of a stone sheepfold perched on the top of a knoll. The best views of it are from the eastern slopes of the valley, where you can look down on the fold with a tiny shepherd's cot built into one corner. The enclosure was built sometime after the severe snow storms in 1878, when the shepherd Robert Little recorded that 292 sheep died on the night of 28 March.

The path continues along the west bank of Hoaroak Water and in half a mile you come to the Hoar Oak Tree and the Forest boundary. Below the boundary wall is Brendon Common where you may well see a herd of Exmoor ponies. In the summer ring ouzels and wheatears nest in the valley. Hoar Oak Tree, and the now vanished Kite Oak in Chalk Water were two of the old Forest boundary markers. It is known that a Hoar Oak Tree 'full of great age and rottenness' fell in 1658, and its successor in December 1916. The present tree was planted in January 1917. 'Hoar' like the village Oare on the Somerset–Devon border, is a Saxon word for boundary.

Hoar Oak to Chapman Barrows – 5 miles

This is the long homeward leg where the route turns to the left and follows the Knight boundary wall on its northern side up over the edge of Furzehill Common and down into Ruckham Combe, headwaters of the West Lyn river. Still keeping to the wall the track goes on to Saddle Gate, a name only on the map for the Saddle Stone (a boundary marker) has long disappeared. From the commons and villages of nearby Parracombe, Lynton, Brendon, and Countisbury shepherds from the sixteenth to nine-teenth centuries, drove their sheep into the Forest for summer grazing and paid the Warden for the right to do so.

The landscape on the Chains has remained unchanged for centuries, but in the 1950s the owners, the Fortescue estate who bought the Forest from the Knights, and the Forestry Commission, came close to changing it completely. They wanted to plant conifers across it. Their plans were resisted only by a vociferous public campaign, a case that reflects the vulnerability of these landscapes. Being in the National Park was in itself no guarantee that this area of outstanding beauty would remain unspoilt but public pressure caused the plans to be dropped. The protesters went on to form the Exmoor Society, a present day watchdog for Exmoor. As you make your way along the final stretch of this walk from Saddle Gate to Chapman Barrows, you can reflect on the fragile hold we have on even the most desolate landscapes.

2. Simonsbath, Warren Farm, Larkbarrow, Tom's Hill, Badgworthy Water, Hoccombe Combe, Brendon Two Gates, Blackpits Gate – 15 miles

This circular trail begins with easy walking following the road to Cloven Rocks and dropping down to the Exe at Warren Bridge. From there the route takes you past Warren Farm and over open moorland rising to 1450 feet to the deserted and ruined farms of Larkbarrow and Tom's Hill. Below to the left is Long Combe with leats cut into the hillside and clearly visible. Then down to Tom's Hill Barrows and the head of Badgworthy Water. A stroll through the upper reaches of Badgworthy Water is delightful. The path runs up Hoccombe Combe and Hoccombe Hill, over Brendon Common to Brendon Two Gates.

This route offers lovely views back to the combes flowing into Badgworthy Water, and as far as Dunkery Beacon. When the road is reached there are similar outstanding panoramas ahead, across Cheriton Ridge and Furzehill Common. This open road running between Simonsbath and Lynmouth must be one of the finest stretches on the whole moor. On a fine evening it is worth lingering to watch the sunset, with views over the moor as far as Holdstone Down and Combe Martin.

The road to Simonsbath brings you to the end of the walk.

Simonsbath to Larkbarrow – 5 miles

Starting point at map reference SS767411

Park your car at Simonsbath. Take the Exford road as far as Cloven Rocks, and then turn left onto the waymarked path. This brings you down to the Exe at Warren Bridge, where you join the road to Warren Farm.

The farmhouse you see today at Warren was built by Frederic Knight. Like so many of his Victorian farmhouses it is built on a sheltered south-facing slope, with superb views over the River Exe. One of the fascinating features of the farm is the four distinct rabbit warrens lying below the farmhouse, also south-facing. No one knows for sure how old these are but Roger Burton has speculated that rabbits could have been bred here as early as the twelfth century, soon after they had been introduced into England by the Normans. This could mean that there was a dwelling here before the present house was built, although it is believed that until the Warden of the Forest, James Boevey, built a house at Simonsbath in 1654 there were no dwellings in the Royal Forest.

Go through the farm and follow the broad path to the right on to the grass moor of Elsworthy. Behind the farm note the remains of John Knight's canal from Exe Head on the left and the bed of the railway from Porlock on the right.

The path continues across the open moor of Elsworthy for almost two miles and leads through a gate on to Swap Hill. Larkbarrow is now a mile away to the north. You can either make straight for the ruined farm and its shelter-belt of battered beeches, or take the path round the head of Long Combe which stretches out below you. Once more there are marvellous views in all directions.

Larkbarrow Farm and the nearby Tom's Hill Farm, were in the centre of a Second World War training area for Allied troops, and suffered severely from shell fire. What the army left standing has now been further reduced by wind and rain. The area has been carefully cleared of explosives. The farms were built in the 1840s by the Knights and various tenants tried in vain to make the farms pay. But when you stand in the ruins and look at what remains of the gardens and attempts to enclose the moor you cannot help but admire the pioneering spirit of people struggling with a hostile landscape.

Across the valley you can see a good example. From near the springhead of Long Combe a leat runs along the south side of the combe and opposite Tom's Hill there is a second leat. These were constructed to irrigate the grass slopes in the early spring, to give an early bite of grass for the stock. Today the area is owned by the National Park who have a herd of pure-bred Exmoor ponies running here. Some grazing is also let for sheep and cattle.

Larkbarrow to Badgworthy – 2 miles

The path from Larkbarrow through Tom's Hill to Badgworthy is wide and clear. In the bottom of the combe beyond Tom's Hill and near the junction of the East Pinford stream with Long Combe, there is a sheep 'stell'. This one is round with a small stone and earth wall, about 3 feet high with some old hawthorns on the top. The stell was introduced to Exmoor by William Little, one of the Scottish shepherds whom Frederic Knight brought to Exmoor, along with their sheep, in the 1870s. William Little first took charge of the shepherding at Pinkery but he moved to Tom's Hill in 1898 to take over the double herding at Larkbarrow. He farmed Tom's Hill until he retired in 1925, in his 70s. He kept extensive notebooks about the herdings and the Knight estate and a lot of what is known about the nineteenth century 'improvement' on Exmoor must be credited to him.

Two incidents show just how hazardous life could be for the farming community in those days. In 1881, Adam Dunn, a shepherd living in Larkbarrow, died of exposure having fallen unconscious on his way home from a night of drinking, and in 1923 Will Little, the son of William, was living in Larkbarrow Cottage when he was struck and killed by lightning.

Returning to the path you drop down in half a mile to Tom's Hill Barrows (which are not manmade, but large natural mounds) and the start of Badgworthy Water, an area made famous by R. D. Blackmore in *Lorna Doone*. This is a beautiful and quiet spot, a place for rest and any food you have carried.

Look out for the wheatears and whinchats that nest amicably on the barrows.

Badgworthy Water is formed by the junction of Long Combe and Hoccombe Water (not to be confused with the adjacent Hoccombe Combe). It marks the Somerset–Devon border and it is possible to walk down the water for three miles to Malmsmead, a tourist centre where the car parks are full in summer and the Doone industry flourishes. Even the Ordnance Survey maps name the area 'Doone Country'. At Malmsmead there is also a natural history field centre run by the Exmoor Natural History Society with displays, a book stall and conducted walks on Wednesday afternoons from May to September.

Cross the river by the not so beautiful but handy wooden footbridge and before taking the path alongside Badgworthy Water, look down at Hoccombe Water. The dry stone wall is part of John Knight's Forest enclosure. This fine example of dry stone walling is falling down in places. This is a pity for it is quite historic, not only as the Forest wall, but in marking the boundary between Somerset and Devon. It is believed that farmers from Brendon pulled the wall down as John Knight built it, fearful that he intended to extend his territory into Brendon Common. The ruins of a shepherd's cottage in Hoccombe Water are thought by some to have been a look-out post so that Knight's men could keep an eye on the commoners. Looking up Hoccombe Water you can see on the left the characteristic *molinia* grass of the Royal Forest, and on the right the heather of the parish commons.

The course of this walk follows Badgworthy Water downstream for nearly a mile and passes a combe with a small heronry. It crosses a stream by a beech hedge and turns left into Hoccombe Combe, whilst the path to Malmsmead carries on down Badgworthy Water.

Behind the mound guarding the entrance to Hoccombe Combe is the site of a deserted hamlet, perhaps the fictional Doone settlement pictured in *Lorna Doone*. What is known about it is that in 1400 the land and property belonged to Lord Harrington, Lord of the Manor of Brendon. The bailiff's accounts reveal there was a farm, cottages, and a priest, but by 1430 the place was deserted.

One man who has looked closely at the remains is Dr Ernest Mold of Lynton. He says, 'There is clear evidence on the ground to show that a number of longhouses existed here at one time. You can see how they might have worked. They run east to west on a slope with the family living at the upper end and the stock, cattle or pigs, down wind and close to the water. There was certainly a community here. Higher up the hill there is evidence that a church existed and higher still there would certainly have been a burial ground. My own guess, and it is only a guess, is that the village was probably inhabited until the Black Death when it probably could not survive and was abandoned.'

Badgworthy Water to Blackpits Gate and Simonsbath – 8 miles

As you begin the climb up through Hoccombe Combe you pass the site of another ruined cottage, Badgworthy Cottage. This is of much later date. A photograph taken in the 1890s shows it had a slate roof with 'Teas' written across it. But no teas today, for it was yet another victim of wartime military training.

Just beyond the ruins of the cottage the path divides, that to the right heading for Lankcombe Ford and Dry Bridge and to the left to the Simonsbath to Lynton road near Brendon Two Gates. You should not leave the area without taking a look at the Bronze Age cairn to the right of the path on Badgworthy Lees. On the top of the hill is a stone entrance to what Ernest Mold believes to be a cemetery. It certainly has that feel about it, and beyond it and aligned on it are a single standing stone, a small barrow and a second stone. One cannot escape the feeling that we are in the midst of some Bronze Age community. This feeling is enhanced by the existence of two long stone rows on the other side of the valley. There must have been a settlement here that goes back 3000 years. Perhaps the standing stones and the cairn had ceremonial significance for the ancient inhabitants. Perhaps the stone rows were similarly significant, but we know so little about their everyday lives. We can only speculate. If you want to roam around these sites it is worth bearing in mind that winter is a better time than summer. In the summer the bracken

Sante Lafuente cutting peat

'Most peat digging goes on in spring because you need dry, fine, windy weather and rain is terrible. You take off the top layer, place it carefully on a dug bed so that it will grow again. You dig out the spits and lay them out. They take ten days to dry, then you turn them over. After another week they will be bone hard, just like coal, and very good for your fire.

I came to England in 1937 when I was 14 years old. Before that I lived in San Sebastian in Spain. The town was heavily bombed, German planes coming over and over so they thought they'd evacuate as many of the youngsters as they could. They put about five thousand into a transatlantic boat, the Havana, and we landed at Southampton in May.

I didn't like it much, I got very seasick and I was very homesick when I got here, but it's a good country to live in. I had three brothers killed in the Civil War and one who managed to get over to France. I have no others in Spain now.'

and long grasses conceal much of the evidence, but winter exposes them beautifully.

If you take the left hand track you will cross Hoccombe Combe on to Brendon Common and then drop down into Hoccombe Water. This has a number of damp spots but is excellent for bog plants. The track over Hoccombe Hill, which is well used but not a right of way, leads to Brendon Two Gates. There are no gates here today, just a cattle grid. At one time two gates hung from a single post and opened in opposite directions, so that no matter which way the wind blew it would always blow one gate shut. Ingenious, as were the local children, who used to collect pennies from riders by opening the gates for them. It is possible to turn left at Brendon Two Gates and walk back to the start of the walk via the road. This is about 3 miles of quite respectable road walking. On this route you may also see evidence of peat cuttings on Lanacombe.

One of the men who digs peat for himself and others is Sante Lafuente. He reckons on digging about 1500 spits on a good day. He designed the spade for the job himself, keeping it sharp with a blade sharpener he carries with him on site. Sante came to England in 1937 from San Sebastian in Spain, a child refugee from the Fascist attacks on his home during the Civil War in that country. He moved to Exmoor and lives in Simonsbath.

An alternative is to carry on west across Brendon Common following the Forest wall as far as Hoaroak Water. By the famous Hoar Oak Tree, cross the water and turn left up the valley. It is beautiful walking in one of Exmoor's most remote areas. You pass the sheepfold high to your right and then cross the stream from Long Chains Combe. The path then rises steeply back on to the Chains at Exehead, the source of the river from which Exmoor takes its name. Turn left here and follow the path eastwards by the young Exe to Blackpits Gate and the Simonsbath to Lynton road.

When you meet the road turn right and walk back up the hill towards Simonsbath where this long walk started. Over four thousand acres of land around here were bought from the Fortescue Estate by the National Park in 1991. This will open up new paths and greater opportunities for walking in the Old Royal Forest of Exmoor.

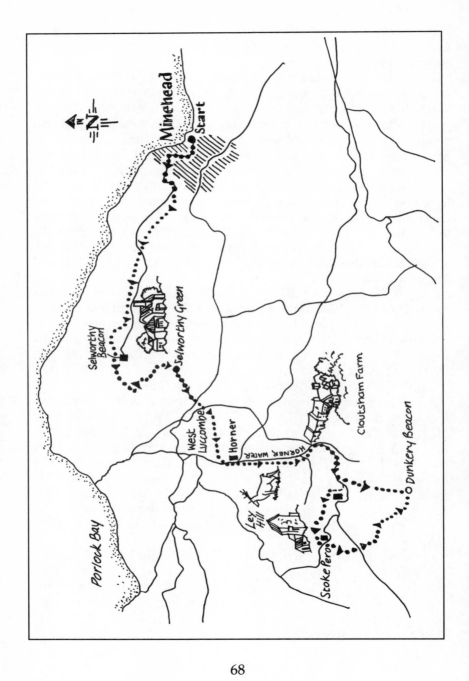

Minehead

Start

Selworthy Beacon

Selworthy Green

Porlock Bay

West Luccombe

Horner

HORNER WATER

Cloutsham Farm

Ley Hill

Stoke Pero

Dunkery Beacon

6

MINEHEAD TO DUNKERY

Minehead to Dunkery via North Hill, Selworthy Green, Horner Wood, Cloutsham and Stoke Pero – 14 miles

Starting point at map reference SS975464

Walkers who arrive at Minehead by steam train first see North Hill standing like a giant buffer at the end of the line. The coastal path hairpins up the hill through Culver Woods on the steeps above the harbour, but a gentler ascent is possible via Wood Combe on the south side of the hill. Make for the parish church of St Michael prominent on North Hill. The church is large and speaks of a prosperous medieval community based on fishing, trading and farming. Below it, the thatched cottages of Higher Town tumble in artless but beautiful confusion down Church Steps.

Beyond the church the road to North Hill turns sharp left and then right. Shortly afterwards three paths go off to the left. Take the first of these and bear right at each of the subsequent two junctions which brings you to the path that follows the contour around the top of Wood Combe. Down on the valley bottom, between North Hill and the heights of Hopcott Common opposite, waves of development are still breaking further and further inland. The straight lines and severe shapes of early post-war

The Station-master, Minehead

housing give way to the whorls and eddies of little closes in which contemporary planners are clearly trying to re-create that sense of community which their previous efforts have done so much to extinguish.

William and Dorothy Wordsworth passed this way on their walks from the Quantocks to Lynmouth in the last years of the eighteenth century. In his later *Guide to the Lakes*, Wordsworth addressed himself to 'wealthy purchasers' who intended to build in unspoilt places, urging them to 'prevent unnecessary deviations from that path of simplicity and beauty along which, without design and unconsciously, their humble predecessors have moved.' The terms of his appeal are re-stated – and refuted – in the contrast between Higher Town and the new town of suburban Minehead.

The path dips into the combe and then rises again. At the top, turn left and take the path that runs parallel to the metalled road – a legacy of defence activity during the Second World War. A level walk of two miles or so leads to the summit. On the way there are fine views to be had in every direction. To the north can be seen the coast of South Wales; hardly visible in bad weather; a hazy presence much of the rest of the time; but on some days so clear that single fields can be picked out on the other side. North-west, along the Bristol Channel, lie the Somerset Levels and the Mendips – the cut-off cone of Brent Knoll prominent to landward, the bluff cliffs of Steep Holm island standing guard off Weston-super-Mare. Here, so local legend has it, lies the buried treasure of pirate Henry Morgan. Going west, the hills of Exmoor fall into the sea – at Culbone and Glenthorne and Foreland Point. It is a wild and desolate shore that has attracted stories of outcast colonies – of criminals and lepers and wreckers – none of them, alas, with any historical foundation. And to the south 'the purple headed mountain' of Dunkery Beacon broods over all.

Each season adds its colours to the palette of these panoramas. Each has its admirers, but the late summer flowering of purple heather and vibrant yellow gorse flowers that carpet North Hill from end to end has few equals in the Exmoor year. The birds of this coastal heath include stonechats, whinchats, linnets, skylarks and meadow pipits, and on the rocky parts wheatears.

Selworthy Beacon crowns the hill with a pile of stones. When clouds shrouded the higher peak of Dunkery, a secondary beacon was lit here to warn of invasion from the sea, or to celebrate national good news. Two paths run west from the Beacon. The left hand one leads down to the head of Selworthy Combe. There stands a tiny redstone memorial hut, drily tiled and adorned on all four sides with seats and inscriptions.

> 'Needs no show of mountain hoary
> Winding shore or deepening glen
> Where the landscape in its glory
> Teaches truth to wandering men.'
> John Keble: *The Christian Year* (1827).

The hut was built in 1871 to the memory of Sir Thomas Acland, Bart. We are standing on Acland land. The whole of our walk to Dunkery is over Acland land in the shape of the Holnicote Estate. Aclands of the eighteenth century were alleged to be able to walk across Devon from the Bristol Channel to the English Channel without leaving their own property.

Sir Thomas – the tenth baronet – was sometimes known as the Great Sir Thomas, and as we wind our way down the Combe through firs and larch and beech and birch and oak we can reflect on the historic trajectory of the English land-owning classes that is exemplified in his life. Until the end of the eighteenth century the Aclands – who acquired Holnicote through marriage to Elizabeth Dyke – led the life of the archetypal sporting squirearchy, hunting deer and the fox, and entertaining on a scale that threatened to exhaust their rental incomes. Starting with Great Sir Thomas a new seriousness entered their conduct – a life of Christian witness and public service in local and national politics took the place of hunting and entertaining. To celebrate the birth of each of his children, Sir Thomas planted a block of trees on the slopes of North Hill. He had a lot of children, and the moor gradually disappeared beneath a frieze of mixed and colourful woodland.

At the bottom of the combe nestles the hamlet of Selworthy Green – a knot of pretty thatched cottages around an open space beside a splashing brook. Built by Sir Thomas for his estate

View towards Dunkery from Selworthy church porch

Sir Richard Acland *(courtesy of Ann, Lady Acland)*

pensioners, the green is an early example of social housing. In 1944 his great great grandson Sir Richard Acland – a christian socialist and founder of the wartime Common Wealth party – gave the whole of his estates including Holnicote to the National Trust.

'Would it not be rather wonderful to live in a world in which we did not all have to think about ourselves all the time? Would it not be rather wonderful to get away from "this is mine", "this is yours", "this is the other fellows," and look out on everything we saw and say "this is all ours?"' Richard Acland: *Unser Kampf* (Penguin, 1940).

Now Selworthy Green is a tourist attraction. One of the cottages serves teas in summer and another has been transformed into a pomander-scented shop selling National Trust artefacts.

Selworthy church, distinctively whitewashed on the outside, has Acland features inside including an unusual family pew over the porch. The view across Porlock Vale through the arch of the south door must be one of the best to be seen anywhere in England. Note the filigree carving of the south aisle roof and the figurative bosses on the timbers of the nave roof. The leather-tooled narrative panels behind the altar were made by Philip Burgess – a member of the famous Porlock leatherwork class, 1900–1912. In the churchyard the yew tree near the tower was planted by Sir Thomas Acland in 1860 to mark his 73rd birthday; the one on the other side was planted at the same time by the rector the Reverend Joshua Stephenson on his 90th.

Descend from Selworthy and cross over the main Minehead – Porlock road, turning left then immediately right around the edge of the estate yard of Holnicote House – now the National Trust Offices. The house itself has been much rebuilt and is used as a residential holiday centre. Presently the path crosses a stream and a minor road and proceeds via fields dotted with mature trees to emerge above Horner. There are two packhorse bridges just here across the Horner Water – one to the right at West Luccombe, and the other to the left. Horner village offers more refreshment (non-alcoholic) for the traveller before the climb begins through the wooded valleys that skirt Dunkery. There is also ample car parking and toilets – but oddly no sign of a public telephone – which make it a popular starting point for shorter walks.

Horner Wood has 900 acres of ancient oak and is full of interest to the naturalist. Red deer abound and can often be seen from the paths. They tend to spend the early morning grazing on moorland at Ley Hill, or farmland at Cloutsham, and to take cover along the edges of the woodland during the day. Although they have grown used to the presence of people they will not permit too close an approach. Patience and some elementary woodcraft makes the stalking of these dignified and secretive animals with camera or binoculars a most satisfying pastime.

But although the deer are numerous enough to make sightings commonplace there are distinct threats to the good health of the Exmoor herd. There may be too many of them, for a start, and the proportion of mature stags may be too low to ensure vigorous breeding. The autumn rut, an annual sexual spectacle, when bellowing stags – locally they call it 'balveing' – compete for the hinds, is now almost non-existent. There are so many hinds and so few stags that little or no competition is necessary.

Bird life is prolific in the woodland. There are three resident species of woodpeckers, the nuthatch, treecreeper, tawny owl, stock dove, jackdaw, jay and buzzard, and the summer visitors include the wood warbler, redstart and pied flycatcher. Sixty nest boxes are maintained here by the Exmoor Natural History Society – and are much used.

Although flowering plants are sparse under the deep shade of the oaks, Horner Wood is rich in non-flowering plants: fungi, lichens, and ferns. The red and white caps of the poisonous fly agaric toadstool contrast with the tiny white strands of the candle-snuff fungus, so called from its similarity to a snuffed out candle-wick. There are more than 200 lichens including *usnea* specie from which a non-allergic antibiotic can be extracted, and the lungwort, formerly used in the treatment of tuberculosis. Polypody ferns decorate the branches of the old oak trees, and on the ground beneath grow fronds of broad-buckler, soft shield, lady, scaly-male and other ferns.

Where the stream divides, follow the path to the left along the floor of the East Water Valley. Watch out here for dippers and grey wagtails and the herons which fish the stream for brown trout. The valley curves round to the right, past oak trees that the National Trust have recently started to pollard, and meets the road by a ford where the downflow from Aller Combe pours into East Water. There is car parking in the field alongside the river – a favourite picnic spot below Cloutsham Farm.

There is a choice of routes at this point. One path crosses the picnic field and begins to climb Dunkery along the edge of Aller Combe, passing beneath the fortified wall of an Iron Age ring fort at Sweetworthy – 'Sweetery' to the locals. Still further west, in Bagley Combe, are traces of a Saxon settlement recorded in the Domesday.

An alternative route goes up the other side of the valley to Cloutsham. Two tracks to the right of the road – one of them a nature trail – lead up to the farm. Once a hamlet of houses stood here. Now only the farm and its outbuildings remain, looking out across the wooded valley to the lower slopes of Dunkery. Tenants of the National Trust have kept sheep and cattle on this land, have tolerated grazing deer in their fields, and for many years have also welcomed bed and breakfast visitors to the house. In the later nineteenth century the Acland family built a Swiss chalet style balcony on the gable end of the farm, and used the accommodation as a summer house, for convalescence, and for honeymoons.

Behind the farm a path crosses the fields and skirts around the upper edge of the wooded Horner valley, across Prickslade Combe and through Stoke Wood to Stoke Pero. Here another fine farmhouse cosies up to a minuscule moortop church. The church is ancient but is not – as the notice on the gate proclaims – in the Domesday Book. Inside, the church is neat and sweet in the refurbished Victorian manner, but its most intriguing feature is its tower – the oldest part of the building. It is pierced by a deep peep-hole of a window inside which wild ferns flourish. Outside, the tower is capped by a saddleback roof that would do credit to a cowshed. At some time in its past the top of the fourteenth-century tower, and its troublesome flat lead roof, have been taken off and replaced with this practical but silly little titfer.

We raise our hats in reply and pass on to the moor above.

77

Bringing in the sheep to be dipped, Cloutsham Farm

Instead of turning left with the road above the church, strike across the moor – first of all by the marked path, and then by open moorland over Stoke Ridge to reach the road and the path beyond at the top of Bagley Combe. Follow the path over Goosemoor Common – a reference to customary grazing rights which have shrunk over the years to a handful of presentday tenants who put sheep and cattle on the hill – until it meets the path almost at the summit of Dunkery. The end of our journey is in sight.

Turn left along the ridge. To the right is a group of Bronze Age burial mounds – Great Rowbarrow and Little Rowbarrow amongst them – that triangulate with the How Cairns and with Dunkery Beacon itself at the apex of the formation. The ground cover is of typical high moorland plants, heather and whortleberry and grasses. As recently as 1970, Exmoor guidebooks also made mention of the native black grouse on Dunkery. There was a shooting syndicate in existence at that time that shot them in season. Now they are all shot out. The last sighting of black grouse was in 1980 and subsequent attempts to re-introduce the species have failed. The red grouse, once common on Dunkery, is now also reduced to just a few pairs. Birds which continue to flourish in this area include curlew, snipe, ring ouzel, stonechat and cuckoo.

A short walk and at last we are arrived at Dunkery – 1704 feet above sea level. On clear days – so they say – the Malvern Hills can be seen to the north and Brown Willy on Bodmin to the south-west. Even on less bright days the views remain spectacular. Dunkery derives its name from the Celtic Dun Creagh meaning 'rough hill' and the description is apt. At this place in past times were lit great beacons. More recently bonfires have illuminated the night sky to commemorate coronations and royal jubilees.

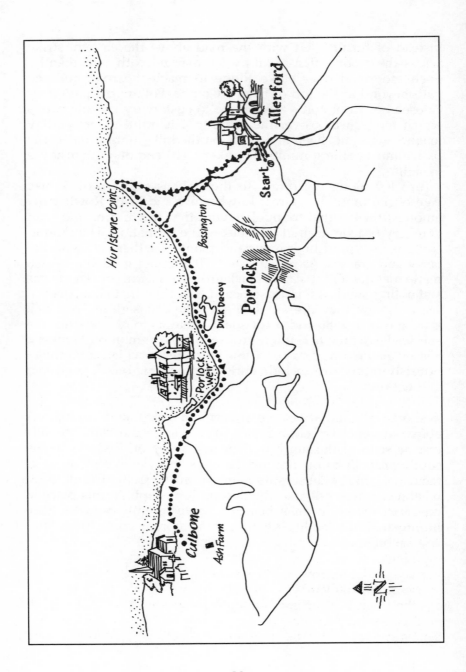

7

PORLOCK VALE

Allerford to Culbone via Bossington, Hurlstone Point, Porlock Weir – 8 miles

Starting point at map reference SS905468

Allerford – with its bridge and its ford and its timeless buildings – is everyone's picture of an English village. A rural paradise perfectly preserved for tourists to snap. Ducks glide and bob in the shallows above the bridge; the stream rushes through on its way to the sea. We follow at a more measured pace along the road leading through the village. Opposite the community hall is the old village school building which has been converted into a local history museum. Next to the school is a pair of brick built workshops. One previously housed a carpenter. The other is a forge. Until Michaelmas Day 1991 this was worked by Fred Kent whose family have carried on the craft of blacksmith in Allerford for more than two hundred years. Fred remembers twenty horses lined up outside the smithy. 'It was first come first served in those days – so they all turned up at six in the morning!'

To avoid the narrow road to Bossington, take the tarmac track on the right, 100 yards beyond the school. This soon peters out but the track is clear enough and crosses the Aller Water by a footbridge. Turn left here along the lively river past a hedgerow that is home to spindle, barberry, holly, hazel and wych elm.

Fred Kent, retired blacksmith, Allerford

Follow the signposts to Bossington and Lynch and this will bring you out on to the road by a medieval chapel-of-ease. The early history of Lynch chapel is not known but it was probably built around 1500. The large east window is identical to those in the south aisle of the parish church of Selworthy. For many years the chapel was closed and used as a barn by the adjoining Lower Lynch Farm until restored in 1885 by Sir Thomas Acland. The farm itself is a marvelously intact group of medieval buildings; linhays with open fronts and grassy thatches supported by round stone pillars.

A little further on, a road arrives from the left past a modest Methodist church built in the style of a westcountry barn. The road comes from Porlock across the rich alluvial plain of the Vale. Until very recently prize-winning malt barley was grown here for brewing. Nowadays nitrates assist a richer crop of winter wheat to flourish, and the barley is little more than a memory and a handful of silver cups on farmhouse sideboards.

Bossington is, if anything, even more picturesque than Allerford. The stone and thatch cottages along the street sport chimneys that climb up the outside walls and end in round stone shapes that echo those of the linhays. Shelves and ledges and daintily-roofed circular protuberances further decorate the buildings. The round features are bread ovens built into the backs of the chimneys. Chimneys like these tell their own history of English vernacular architecture. Medieval houses tended to have no upper stories and the smoke from their fires exited through simple holes in the roof. As the cash economy grew and possessions multiplied and, as people began to prize a measure of privacy, chimneys were an invention that permitted better use to be made of spaces inside houses. They also allowed householders to make public statements of their wealth. The height of many old chimneys is partly due to this kind of display, but it also served the practical purpose of lifting sparks away from the thatch.

Alongside the road, bordered here and there by a cobbled pavement, runs a leat or stream that passes under the ends of several houses. The rooms above the stream were the dairies, and the stream cooled the slate floors and the milk churns that stood on them. No milk is stored here today. There is still a working farm but the village street shouts with bed and breakfast signs and a cafe. Tourism is today's summer harvest in Bossington.

An alternative route to the far end of Bossington village is to cross the bridge at Lynch just before the chapel-of-ease and to find the path that crosses the fields below the woods planted by Sir Thomas Acland. Amongst the trees there are stands of evergreen holm oak.

As it approaches Bossington the path descends a wooded cliff above the noisy confluence of two rivers – the Horner and the Aller – that join forces and push on down to the not-too-distant sea. From the car park at the north end of Bossington, cross the river by the wooden footbridge and follows the sign to Hurlstone Point. A gently rising path passes marshy ponds to the left; beyond them the shingle bank of Porlock beach; and beyond that the edge of the Atlantic.

Hurlstone points a stony finger across the Bristol Channel. On it stands the hollow box of what was once the coastguards' lookout – roofless, floorless, windowless. Local volunteers kept a bad-weather watch from here for almost seventy years. Now they only come to practice cliff rescue techniques on the precipitous cliffs beyond the lookout. The cliff-walk past the ruin has been fenced off. Experienced walkers with heads for height can proceed towards Minehead this way but only in good weather. Strong winds are a great danger to walkers on this part of the route. Rounding the first bend brings rewards in the form of views into a rocky bay with the moors of North Hill above.

Wales fills the horizon to the north. Across these narrow straits there came, in the sixth century AD, a succession of Celtic saints bearing the message of Christianity and establishing the first Christian sites in pagan England. They are remembered in a litany of church names along this coastline – St Petroc at Parracombe, St Decuman at Watchet, St Beuno at Culbone, and St Dubricius at Porlock.

Porlock itself stands back from the present-day beach on an incline that may have been the shore in times past. Its name means the 'locked port', although whether the harbour was open in Saxon times is not known. Fertile fields fill most of the space behind the beach. Further west they give way to wetlands and waving reeds.

Walk back down the path from Hurlstone. To the right is a steep path to the east end of the beach. At low tide it is possible to pass below the Point through a natural arch in the rock formation called the Gull Hole. But it is difficult due to the sharp shelled barnacles on the rocks and can be dangerous since a retreat must be made before the tide begins to come in. Herring gulls live on these cliffs and for more than a hundred years ravens have nested here.

Shingle makes for heavy going – a mile of this is worth two on firm ground. But at most places it is possible to descend onto the drained land behind the stones. Half a mile along the beach Horner Water ends in a pool that drains through the bank into the sea. At high tides and after heavy rain the waters of the Horner break through the stones, but the tide soon refurbishes the barrier. At this spot the remains of a substantial lime kiln are to be seen. This was an Acland Estate enterprise dating from the eighteenth century. Coal and limestone were brought in boats from South Wales and dumped over the side at high water. As the tide receded the materials were recovered from the beach and fed into the kiln. The resulting lime was used as fertiliser on the fields of Porlock Vale and the nearby hills of Exmoor.

Flanking the ruins of the kiln buildings are two pillboxes – parts of the coastal defence work of the Second World War. The threat of invasion from the sea caused the construction of a chain of pillboxes that stretched from Burnham on Sea in the north to Seaton on the south coast – effectively barring the way out of the South West peninsula. Subsidiary defences ran along the north Somerset coast as far as here – and then stopped. The cliffs of Exmoor beyond Porlock need no defending. Care was taken to disguise the defensive positions to blend in with their surroundings. Oliver Messel, the stage designer, is said to have turned his hand to this branch of martial art – at Minehead the pillboxes were constructed to look like seafront shelters and public lavatories. On Porlock beach they are faced with pebbles like those on which they stand.

Other memories of war also invest this shore. In the First World War German submarines penetrated the waters of the Bristol Channel and sank ships off Porlock. In 1940 a German Junkers bomber came down on the beach – three of the crew survived, but flight engineer Wilhelm Ruehl is buried in the local churchyard. Beside the path is a stone monument to twelve American airmen who died when their Liberator bomber crashed into the marsh in 1942, killing all but one of the crew.

Halfway along the curve of the bay is an area of salt marsh. Amongst the prolific flora of this habitat are to be found salt-marsh rushes and grasses, sea arrowgrass, orache, sea aster, sea-spurry and the tiny glasswort plant once used in the production of glass. The shingle supports yellow horned poppy and ever-lasting pea, whilst the rhines and ditches provide habitat for yet another range of plants including the amphibious bistort, at home both on land and afloat on water.

Clearly marked on many old maps is 'The Decoy' – a device for trapping ducks. A long pond was made, at one end of which a blind tunnel made of branches was constructed. The ducks were driven along the channel and into the tunnel from which there was no escape and there they were killed – for food and feathers. Now only the outline of the pond remains, but the area still provides an important feeding and resting place for migrant and other birds. Species nesting here include reed and sedge warblers, redshank, lapwing, and shelduck. Birdwatchers can come here expecting the unexpected: bittern, little egret, avocet, grey phalarope and other rarities have all been recorded here in recent years. The reedbed provides cover and nest sites for birds and is cut and harvested in a small way by the Blathwayt Estate for use in thatching.

Further on there are ruins that commemorate an occasion when nature fought back against other plans for human domination. In 1910 a golf course was planned and constructed complete with is own clubhouse. The great storm of that year came over the shingle and swept the whole thing away – for ever.

Porlock Weir is our next port of call – a tiny fishing and trading dock with high lock gates, that now mostly harbours leisure craft, although two fishermen still work the local waters for herring and tourists. The Weir was also the destination of an epic boat journey of the nineteenth century – the overland launch of the Lynmouth lifeboat on the night of the 12 January, 1899. The *Louisa* was thirty-six feet long, seven foot six wide, and weighed three and a half tons unladen. Giant seas meant that it could not be launched at Lynmouth to go to the aid of a three-masted ship dragging its anchor in Porlock Bay. With the help of eighteen horses the life-boat was towed up one of the steepest hills in England, along ten miles of wild moorland road, and down the daunting decline of Porlock Hill. In the event the sailors and the schooner would have been saved without the assistance of Lynmouth boat, but the audacity and endurance of the launch live on as testaments to the ordinary and everyday heroism of the crew. A thrilling account of the event is contained in *The Overland Launch* by C. Walter Hodges (Exmoor Books).

Refreshments of all kinds are to be had at the Weir. Seize the opportunity to take in extra energy as the path ahead is steeply upward. We are going to climb nearly six hundred feet to one of the secret places of early Christianity in this country.

Pass along the front of the Anchor Hotel and the converted buildings beyond it. The path is signposted to the left up a flight of steep steps. Continue across the fields. At the Worthy toll take the path that goes right through the gate just before the house. There is a sign to Culbone. To begin with the path runs through mysterious cuttings and tunnels surmounted by walls and steps and lookout-posts. All of these workings and buildings represent attempts by the garden landscapers of Ashley Combe house to disguise the passage of the footpath through its grounds and to provide unbroken access to the sea. The house – now gone – was home to Lord Byron's daughter Ada, in the early nineteenth century.

Higher up, the path is clearly barred off and diverted onto an even steeper part of the slope. The Exmoor National Park which owns this part of the coast has re-routed the path to avoid the place where an entire section of the hillside has slipped into the sea. The bedding planes here incline steeply down toward the Bristol Channel and a further huge mass of earth and vegetation is visibly preparing to detach itself from the rocks.

The path winds on through woodland for almost two miles with occasional glimpses of the sea far below. Among the trees grow a number of naturalised strawberry trees, native of Mediterranean lands and also of south-west Ireland, but rare in the wild in Britain. The tree, growing up to 30 feet high with a peeling, reddish bark, is our largest member of the heather family. The cream coloured flowers open in early winter, and the warty fruit, much like a medium sized strawberry, ripens in the autumn of the following year.

At Culbone, safely lodged on a diminutive plateau between the walls of the combe, is the ancient church of St Beuno. When the Reverend Richard Warner visited Culbone church in 1799 he described, 'Two cottages, planted just without the consecrated ground – its only companions in this secluded dell.' The two cottages still survive, and in the lower one lived Lizzie Cook. For 65 years until her death at the age of 90, she dispensed tea and information to countless visitors. Built as a monastic retreat in the eremitic tradition of the Celtic saints Culbone is the smallest complete Anglican church in England and has many interesting features. On the north wall are two windows that merit more than a passing look. One is a tiny slit about three feet above ground level. It is known as the leper's window because of its size and location and the fact that the altar can be sighted through it from the outside. It is plausible that lepers who were excluded from human contact could have observed the offices through this window – but there is no way of verifying this from historical sources.

The second window is thought to date from Saxon times and consists of a double-pointed arch with a grotesquely featured face carved into the space between the two arches. It could be a 'green man' – a figure representing the primeval forces of nature that appears in church architecture throughout Europe – but there is no sign of the usual telltale foliage around the face of this one.

The churchyard is filled with headstones bearing local names. The Richards and the Reds – and the wonderfully symmetrical name of Richard Red Richards, an award-winning malt-barley farmer from the Vale of Porlock – who joined the two families in marriage.

Above the combe where Culbone stands, a semi-circle of farmsteads cling to the steep side of the hill and vie with each other

Saxon window, Culbone church

for the right to claim that the romantic poet Samuel Taylor Coleridge wrote his renowned fragment *Kubla Khan* whilst staying there. Ash Farm is generally reckoned to be his lodging place, but there is no exact record. In the midst of writing, Coleridge was interrupted by the infamous 'person from Porlock', after whose visit the muse had fled, taking with it the unwritten portion of his poem.

There is no public access to the farm from the church.

Coleridge was wont to walk up Culbone en route from Nether Stowey to Lynmouth – sometimes in the company of his friends Dorothy and William Wordsworth. So we are walking in hallowed footsteps. Along these paths and through these woods there was nurtured and brought to maturity a view of the English countryside that some may dismiss as 'romantic' but which is still the way that most of us 'see' the natural world. Nature was not always seen in this way – in the eighteenth century and earlier it featured in many texts as a wild and inhospitable environment to be tamed and gentled by the hand of man. But in the works of Coleridge and Wordsworth and others it was transformed into something more recognisably modern.

> *Therefore am I still*
> *A lover of meadows and the woods,*
> *And mountain; and of all that we behold*
> *From this green earth; of all the mighty world*
> *Of eye and ear, both what they half create*
> *And what perceive; well pleased to recognise*
> *In nature and the language of the sense,*
> *The anchor of my purest thoughts, the nurse,*
> *The guide, the guardian of my heart, and soul*
> *Of all my moral being.*

William Wordsworth.
Lines composed a few miles above Tintern Abbey.
13 July 1798

Hope Bourne, Exmoor writer

'The great thing about declaring the place a National Park is preserving what is left of its wilderness character. And that I think is the most important thing. There are many areas of beauty and many sorts of beauty, natural and man-made, but the thing that matters here is what is left of the wilderness. It's something I think that we need, we need our roots and our roots are not in civilisation.'

FURTHER READING

Exmoor books currently in print

Allen, N.	*Exmoor Place Names*, Alcombe Books, 1986
	The Waters of Exmoor, Exmoor Press, 1978
	Exmoor's Wild Red Deer, Exmoor Press, 1990
Allen & Butcher	*Birds of Exmoor National Park*, Alcombe Books, 1984
Allen & Giddens	*Exmoor Wildlife*, Exmoor Press, 1989
Binding, H.	*Discovering Dunster*, Exmoor Press, 1990
	Old Minehead and Around, Exmoor Press, 1983
Binding & Bonham-Carter	*Old Dulverton and Around*, Exmoor Press, 1986
Blackmore, R. D.	*Lorna Doone*, various publishers, 1st ed. 1869
Bonham-Carter, V.	*The Essence of Exmoor*, Exmoor Press, 1991
Bourne, H.	*Living on Exmoor*, Exmoor Books, 2nd ed. 1991
Bridle, H.	*Woody Bay*, Merlin Books, 1991
Burton, S. H.	*Exmoor*, Hale, 4th ed. 1984
	The Lorna Doone Trail, Exmoor Press, 1975
Burton, R.	*The Heritage of Exmoor*, Privately Printed, 1989
Exmoor National Park	*Enjoying Exmoor*, E.N.P.A., 1985
Gardner, B.	*Lorna Doone's Exmoor*, Exmoor Press, 1990
Giddens, C.	*Flowers of Exmoor*, Alcombe Books, 1977
Hurley, J.	*Exmoor in Wartime*, Exmoor Press, 1978
	Murder and Mystery on Exmoor, Exmoor Press, 4th ed. 1982
Lawrence, B.	*Exmoor Villages*, Exmoor Press, 1984
Robbins, J.	*The Moths & Butterflies of Exmoor National Park*, Alcombe Books, 1990
Eardley-Wilmot, H.	*Ancient Exmoor*, Exmoor Press, 1983
	Yesterday's Exmoor, Exmoor Books, 1990